Contents

Acknowledgements

Clearly, a project of this size can only emerge after many years of reflection on one's own and other people's work and as a result of dialogue with colleagues working in the same field.

While taking full responsibility for what is written here, we acknowledge our indebtedness to all those people who have stimulated our reflection and joined us in a continuing process of critical appraisal of all that we do.

One particular acknowledgment needs special mention. The three-circle model of the R.E. Field of Enquiry used in this book has evolved over several years. It has its genesis in work done in the Regional R.E. Centre (Midlands) by Garth Read and Michael Grimmitt in 1975. Garth Read then shared this model with the Religious Education Curriculum Project Team, of which he was a member, working in the Department of Education, Queensland, Australia. This Australian team published the model in a slightly amended form in 1977.

In this present work, we have again altered and extended the model. More significantly, we have used it both as a definition of appropriate content and as an indication of an appropriate methodology. Our understanding of the approaches to teaching R.E. and the selection and sequencing of topics across the 5 – 16 age range emerge directly out of this model.

The Queensland R.E.C.P. team has given us permission to include in this manual some material which was developed during the time that Garth Read was with them. For this we are most grateful.

We would like to express our sincere thanks to Sue Hasted, our editor, for her encouragement and professional integrity. Our thanks are also due to Marie Butler for typing the manuscript and to Barbara Hill who carried extra duties in the Regional R.E. Centre when writing demands became heavy.

Garth Read
John Rudge
Roger Howarth

Foreword

Westhill began in 1907 as a training centre for professional Christian educators. The then-known principles and theories of education were applied rigorously to the teaching of Christianity in churches. Alongside this concern for church education, Westhill has developed an equally strong tradition for applying educational discipline to R.E. teaching in schools. The College's contribution to initial and in-service training of teachers of religion has therefore been constant for most of the twentieth century. This present volume grows out of that long tradition. The staff of the Regional R.E. Centre based at Westhill offer the 5-16 Project as a stimulus to those who still seek to improve the quality of R.E. in schools. It is their contribution and the authors take full responsibility. As a College, however, we strongly commend it. Parts of it might be seen by some as controversial, but that is the story of development in R.E. May it lead to improved concern for the religious aspect of children's personal growth and provide a richer range of challenges to teachers and children as they examine their own beliefs and values.

G. Benfield
Westhill College
Selly Oak

October, 1985

GENERAL INTRODUCTION

The Westhill Project R.E. 5–16 is part of the work of the Regional R.E. Centre (Midlands). It forms a comprehensive package of materials for use by teachers of Religious Education in both primary and secondary schools. There are three main components in this package and while they are interrelated, each stands on its own and can be used quite independently of the others.

The main Project manual, *How do I Teach R.E.?* sets out to explore the structure of R.E. as a school subject and to show how the general aim of the subject can be translated into classroom practice. It is as much concerned with the question 'How should we teach R.E.?' as it is with the questions 'What should we teach and why?' Thus it provides teachers with clear guidelines for school-based curriculum development in regard to R.E.

The supplementary teacher's manuals offer comprehensive overviews of six world religions: Christianity, Islam, Judaism, Hinduism, Buddhism and Sikhism. A seventh manual is concerned with an approach through 'life themes'. The manuals set out to show how such subjects can be taught in a developmental way through the age range five to sixteen.

The teaching materials embody the principles outlined in the manuals and are designed for use in the classroom. They consist of pupils' books and photopacks:

Pupils' books
Four books accompany each of the supplementary teacher's manuals. They follow the teaching schemes recommended in the manuals and relate to four broad bands of schooling:

  Book 1 – Lower primary (5-8 years)
  Book 2 – Upper primary (9-11 years)
  Book 3 – Lower secondary (12-14 years)
  Book 4 – Upper secondary (15-16 + years)

Photopacks
Each pack of twenty A3 colour photographs relates to one of the supplementary manuals. These pictures illustrate aspects of each religion or a significant life theme as expressed in four different contexts: family life, religious community life, personal life and public life. Background information for teachers is printed on the back of each picture under three headings: a description of the event photographed; its significance as subject matter for R.E.; beliefs being expressed or questions being raised.

Most of the Westhill Project materials stem from an ongoing dialogue between classroom teachers and the authors in the context of in-service courses over a number of years. Where particular teachers have contributed directly to the materials, this is duly acknowledged.

The Westhill Project is not intended as the definitive scheme for teaching R.E. but as a contribution to curriculum development. Many elements of current teaching and much previously published material already in use will be found helpful within the scheme we have outlined. Both the authors and the publishers would welcome comments on the books and photopacks, as well as further examples of good practical work in R.E. which could be considered for publication as part of the Project.

PART ONE

WHAT IS R.E. TRYING TO ACHIEVE?

<u>THE AIM OF RELIGIOUS EDUCATION</u>

This is essentially a practical book, setting out to
show how a general aim for R.E. may be translated
in a consistent way into lessons in the classroom.

<u>THE AIM AND GENERAL PRINCIPLES OF RELIGIOUS EDUCATION</u>

**The principle aim of Religious Education is to help children mature in relation to their own
patterns of belief and behaviour through exploring religious beliefs and practices and related
human experiences.**

THE SEVEN PRINCIPLES OF R.E.

FIRST PRINCIPLE	– Children need to develop their own beliefs and values and a consistent pattern of behaviour
SECOND PRINCIPLE	– R.E. has a particularly important contribution to make to the personal and social development of children
THIRD PRINCIPLE	– In R.E. the role of the teacher is that of educator
FOURTH PRINCIPLE	– As in all other subject areas, the teaching of R.E. must be related to the ages and abilities of the children being taught
FIFTH PRINCIPLE	– R.E. will help children to explore a range of religious beliefs and practices and related human experiences
SIXTH PRINCIPLE	– R.E. makes a major contribution to multicultural education
SEVENTH PRINCIPLE	– R.E. does not make assumptions about, or pre-conditions for, the personal commitments of teachers or children

It may seem presumptuous – even somewhat dogmatic – to begin with such a bald statement, as though the answer to the question 'What is R.E. trying to achieve?' is indisputable. That is not the intention. The purpose in stating this aim here is simply to declare, right at the outset, the kind of R.E. that this manual is promoting. It is not to suggest that this is the only way of stating the aim of R.E., nor to deny that there are other views of the subject, some of which might conflict with the view taken here.

The debate about the nature and aims of the school subject 'R.E.' has been going on for a long time. Teachers who wish to explore this debate, and the way in which thinking about the subject has changed in recent years, may like to refer to some of the books and articles listed in the select bibliography. This manual makes no attempt to enter into this general debate. It does, however, seek to reflect, in practical terms, the most recent thinking about the subject, particularly the kind of developments which find expression in a whole range of new local authority agreed syllabuses.

The agreed syllabus still remains the legal basis for the kind of R.E. that is taught in county schools in England and Wales. This basis is derived from the provisions of the 1944 Education Act. In general terms the Act has ensured that R.E. has remained in the school curriculum and at the same time made possible wide-ranging changes in the way the subject is taught. The syllabuses of Birmingham (1975) and Hampshire (1978) have been particularly influential, and a number of other authorities have more recently either adopted one of these or produced their own. In the decade 1975–1985 fifty-three of the one hundred and six local education authorities in England and Wales replaced their older syllabuses with a new one. Although expressed in different ways, all these new syllabuses share a broadly common thinking about the subject, and embody principles similar to those underlying this manual.

These recent developments in the theory of the subject have not always been complemented by parallel developments in curriculum and classroom practice. Before considering this issue, however, it is only right that the general principles on which this manual is based should be made clear. Here they are stated briefly, with some explanations where necessary, but no attempt is made to argue the case for them in detail. It is hoped that this statement of principles will shed some light on the ways in which the subject is developed.

FIRST PRINCIPLE

Children need to develop their own beliefs and values and a consistent pattern of behaviour.

It is a basic assumption of R.E. that the simple fact of being human confronts us every day with experiences, situations and events to which we have to make responses. The particular responses we make will vary according to a number of factors. One of the most important of these is the complex of attitudes and beliefs which go to make our system of values and outlook on life.

Our beliefs and attitudes, and the kind of behaviour and style of life through which we express them, have in turn been informed and shaped by a variety of influences. Some people will, at an early stage in their lives, acquire or adopt a pattern of belief and behaviour which will remain largely unchanged over the years. Others will be continually assessing, reforming and sometimes changing altogether their system of values and outlook on life. Of course, not everyone will spend their every waking moment wrestling with these issues. Some may appear to give hardly any thought to them. Some may regard them as irrelevant in the light of pressing practical considerations. The capacity to think about them or act upon their responses to them may not be developed to the same extent in all people; and many may find it hard to articulate their views or explain their actions. All human beings are, nevertheless, inevitably involved in acquiring and developing attitudes and behaviour patterns – that is part of what is involved in being human. Having beliefs and acting upon them is one of the most important humanising factors. This is particularly true when people find themselves in a situation where they are forced to make a choice between two alternatives. Some may respond simply on the basis of their own self-interest and initial feelings. Others, however, may choose the less attractive alternative, at whatever personal cost, because it squares with their values and expresses their beliefs. By doing so, they rise above merely instinctive responses, and illustrate their capacity for being genuinely human.

It is also part of being human that we take responsibility for our beliefs and actions and embrace them as our own. This element of responsibility is an important aspect of maturity. It follows that mature human beings will think responsibly about their beliefs and will act upon them in a responsible manner. Here, a distinction can be drawn. On the one hand there are people who simply adhere to beliefs and customs out of habit or because they have inherited them or been indoctrinated into them. On the other hand some people have reflected upon them, proved them on the test-bed of their own experiences and subjected them to the scrutiny of the beliefs and values of others.

Children share with all human beings in this task. They too are involved in the process of becoming mature and responsible people. In the early stages of development others may assume some of these responsibilities for them. Their gradual acceptance of responsibility for themselves in relation to their beliefs, values and actions is a mark of maturation. That is why the principle aim of R.E. stated at the beginning of this section is directed to the gradual development of children as autonomous human beings. While there are important considerations arising from the social context in which they are growing up, and from useful knowledge which they might acquire, the overriding consideration in R.E. is the extent to which the subject contributes to their autonomy.

SECOND PRINCIPLE

R.E. has a particularly important contribution to make to the personal and social development of children.

As children mature, it is important that they assume responsibility for themselves and their own actions, and the beliefs and values from which they stem. It is also important that they are able to act in a responsible way towards others. It is in these two areas of personal and social responsibility that teachers of R.E. have most to contribute to children's development.

This is not, of course, to suggest that R.E. is the sole contributor in these areas of development. The personal and social development of children will take place in a whole range of contexts, of which school is only one and probably not the most important or influential. Family life and parental guidance undoubtedly shape the lives of children, often in subconscious yet profound ways. All kinds of groups – local, religious or interest based – are also influential, as is the particular peer group to which children belong. Children's own experiences will also be a forceful tutor in shaping their outlooks, values and commitments. Most of these learning experiences and situations will be found outside school and will continue well beyond school.

Schools do, however, have an essential role to play in this matter of personal and social development. They provide an educational context in which it may take place. There is no one school subject to which it is confined – least of all to a subject called 'Personal and Social Education'. It often takes place through the hidden or informal curriculum and all subjects as well as all teachers have their own contributions to make. The general ethos of the school and the values it represents have a part to play. Although personal and social education is often linked specifically with areas such as careers, moral, social, health, political and religious education, all subjects contribute.

The area of personal and social education is, moreover, important for all children in school. It should not be reserved for the so-called less able. The notion that those of greater ability are too academically orientated to have time for it is evidence of confused educational priorities.

Within this educational framework, R.E. has a particular contribution to make to personal and social education. It is in the area of helping children to shape and develop their own beliefs, values and attitudes, and to behave responsibly towards others, that R.E. makes its main contribution.

THIRD PRINCIPLE

In R.E. the role of the teacher is that of educator.

As the understanding of the place of R.E. in the school curriculum has changed over the years, so also has the understanding of the role of the teacher of R.E.

As an educator, the teacher of R.E. will be concerned to encourage and promote an open, critical and sympathetic approach to the subject. This implies that the teacher will require just those qualities in his or her approach. It is an approach based on a willingness to enquire and to raise questions without necessarily arriving at firm and conclusive answers. At the same time it requires a commitment to the value and importance of the enquiry and a conviction that it is worthwhile for the teacher as well as the children.

In this approach there will be no question of imposing particular values and beliefs on children though, along with all other teachers, the teacher of R.E. will be concerned to support certain basic educational values and the values represented by the school as a whole. More specifically, teachers of R.E. will be concerned to stimulate interest in the various ways in which beliefs shape and influence people's lives. They will involve children in widening their horizons and deepening their perceptions about the world around them, and encouraging them to reflect on their own outlooks.

The teacher of R.E., therefore, has to tread a difficult path, surrounded by pitfalls. The two most dangerous of these are the one that pushes the subject back towards the instructional model, and the one that removes all elements of controversy from the subject, thus robbing it of its essential relevance. The task of the teacher of this subject calls for the highest professional skills if R.E. is not to degenerate to the level where it becomes an easy target for its detractors.

FOURTH PRINCIPLE

As in all other subject areas, the teaching of R.E. must be related to the ages and abilities of the children being taught.

This educational principle is firmly established as part of the essential understanding which teachers bring to their task. This has not always been the case, and the implications of it have not always been applied in the classroom.

Extensive research in the areas of the cognitive and moral development of children has led to a recognition that adult categories, concepts and attitudes are in many cases quite foreign to a child's perception of things. At one time the thinking in this area tended to suggest that the stages of children's development could be defined fairly clearly and that some kind of linear progression could be observed. More recent thinking has come to recognise the complexity in the process of development. Nonetheless, acknowledgement of the basic stages of children's educational and moral development has become part of the received wisdom of educational theory. It has important implications for the way in which R.E. is taught in schools.

In some areas of the curriculum it is possible to see development in children as taking place by the acquisition of concepts which gradually become more sophisticated. There is a sense in which children need to acquire one particular concept or skill before they can progress to the next. Development of understanding in R.E. takes place in a more subtle and less clearly definable way. That is partly because some of the ideas and concepts which children will come across in R.E. are, by their very nature, imprecise and open to many interpretations and responses. At the same time, when teaching R.E. teachers ought not to fall into the trap of assuming that children cannot grasp some of these concepts.

For this reason teachers at both primary and secondary levels need to have a clear grasp of the essential way in which the subject operates and the ways in which its objectives may be achieved. It is these things which this manual sets out to provide.

FIFTH PRINCIPLE

R.E. will help children to explore a range of religious beliefs and practices and related human experiences.

The aim of the subject also encompasses its main areas of essential content which distinguish it from other subject areas. This is not to suggest that the only difference between R.E. and other subjects is the content or area of knowledge it deals with. It is rather to emphasise the importance of the exploration of the subject's content, or field of enquiry, as the means through which the subject's aim is to be realised.

R.E. in fact draws its content from three main areas which are discussed in the next section. It is inevitable that one of these will deal with particular expressions of belief and practice, especially those enshrined in the great traditional belief systems which are a fundamental part of our human heritage and contemporary life. The exploration of these systems is an essential part of R.E., though not by any means the whole of it. Our model and method for such explorations is set out in Part Two.

It is not the intention here to enter into a discussion about the nature of religion. Definitions of religion are notoriously inadequate, however much light they may throw on some aspects of its nature. In R.E. we are concerned with the more practical question of how children are to make sense of the many ways in which they will encounter religious (and non-religious) belief and practice in their daily lives – in the media, in their local communities or among their friends. The focus is therefore on religion as a living and contemporary aspect of life, rather than as a subject for purely historical study.

Children will inevitably observe around them some of the great diversity of beliefs and commitments by which people live. This variety and diversity is important in R.E. It is desirable that children should understand that matters of belief are often controversial and represent different outlooks and interpretations of human experience. Accurate information and thoughtful understanding in this area are much to be preferred to slogans and propaganda.

Younger children will usually come to explore beliefs and values by observing the way people behave. R.E., however, is not merely a study of the outward forms of religion. It will be concerned with exploring the feelings and attitudes that lie behind the behaviour, and with helping children to appreciate the importance in religion of drama, music, story and symbol, and of the way in which language is used figuratively to express meaning.

In the light of this, the view taken in this manual is that R.E. must include the consideration of different religious and non-religious views and traditions. This emphasis on diversity arises both from the nature of the subject, and from the way in which it is to be taught.

This understanding is to be distinguished sharply from the view sometimes referred to as 'market place religion' – the idea that children are given an objective description of a variety of religions and then encouraged to choose one for themselves. This view is wholly unrealistic and pays no regard to either the desirability or the possibility of such choices, or to the ways in which particular commitments are made.

The exploration of religions is, however, only one aspect of R.E., and the subject is not to be limited simply to the study of religion as a detached, academic exercise. R.E. will only be effective if this exploration of religion is related both to wider human experiences and issues and to the children's own outlooks.

The concern of R.E. with these wider areas is not merely peripheral to the subject but an essential element of it. The recognition of this was probably motivated at first by a desire to make the subject more relevant to the needs and interests of children. Indeed, attempts were made at one stage to demonstrate how an exploration of human experience in depth may lead to religious conclusions. That is not the view taken here. The approach of this manual is to recognise that there is an interrelationship between religion and a range of significant human experiences. An exploration of these related experiences will help children towards a better perception of the religious dimension, and will provide a broader background for informing and developing their own ideas and values. Indeed, we would want to stress that it is only through an exploration of all three areas (religious beliefs and practices, wider human experiences, and children's own outlooks), and of the relationships between them, that the aim of R.E. can be achieved.

SIXTH PRINCIPLE

R.E. makes a major contribution to multicultural education.

The sixth principle set out here is complementary to the second, but needs to be stated in its own right on account of its importance. It stems from the kind of society which forms the context in which R.E. is taught as well as from the principles of the subject itself.

There is a serious, continuing debate about the kind of society in which our children are growing up. It arises partly from social fragmentation, partly from regional and cultural diversity and partly from the absence of any one over-arching set of values to which all or even most subscribe. Some view this as a grave defect and there have been various attempts to impose or, at least, encourage some uniformity. Others see it as a saving grace. It has, however, been widely accepted in theory, if not entirely in practice, that the multicultural and pluralist nature of our society is a welcome and desirable benefit. As such it is a reflection of the shrinking and interdependent world in which we live, and in which 'we must learn to live together as brothers (and sisters!) or we shall perish as fools'. Schools have a part to play in encouraging an understanding of and positive attitude to this kind of multicultural society.

R.E., with its focus on questions of belief and value, attitude and outlook, behaviour and practice, has a major contribution to make in this direction. Along with other subjects, and with the values represented by the school as a whole, R.E. contributes to the development of attitudes which promote and support a harmonious and tolerant society. An essential part of this development is an awareness of, and respect for, the beliefs and ways of life of people whose cultural background and traditions differ from those with which we may be familiar.

The concern for tolerance in a situation of cultural diversity is closely related to the aims and content of R.E. On the one hand, tolerance does imply a genuine readiness to explore the views of others in an open way and with an emphasis on accurate understanding. On the other hand, while seeking to avoid conflict (usually based on prejudice, misinformation, propaganda and aggression), it does encourage controversy based on mutual respect and clarity. Tolerance in the context of R.E. does not imply a watering-down or levelling process through which differences are disregarded, convictions and commitments left unexpressed, and the essential challenge of the subject is reduced to the notion that 'all religions amount to the same thing'. It means encouraging them to be explored in a way which does genuine justice to their distinctiveness in an atmosphere of open enquiry.

Clearly the potential for a well balanced and broadly based R.E. programme is usually much greater in areas and schools where cultural and religious diversity is present at first hand. It must nevertheless be understood that the nature of the subject – and of religion itself – implies that multifaith R.E. is as necessary in culturally monochrome areas as it is in areas of great diversity.

It must also be recognised that many children in county schools will probably have no clearly defined religious background, affiliation or commitment. R.E. cannot begin with any presuppositions about their commitments. The absence of traditional commitments reflects the secular (and, often, urban) aspect of our society. It is at least partly on account of this secular context that religious freedom and tolerance are promoted. This does not mean, as some have asserted, that R.E. must therefore by definition be a secular pursuit. Indeed, it is quite clear that as children explore the great religious traditions they will encounter those beliefs and outlooks which represent a challenge to secular attitudes, just as they will also see secular views as a challenge to religious perspectives.

It is also important to recognise that, while society in Britain today may justifiably be described as both pluralistic and secular, it is the religion of Christianity that has played a major role in shaping and informing many of our cultural values and institutions. This recognition of the place and influence of Christianity in Britain means that its beliefs and practices should comprise an essential element of any R.E. programme.

The prominence given to Christianity must, however, still be contained within a multifaith and multicultural context. There can be no question of religious or cultural superiority within the framework of R.E., and Christianity itself, along with all other traditions, needs to be viewed in the light of its own diversity of belief and practice, which is very considerable.

SEVENTH PRINCIPLE

R.E. does not make assumptions about, or preconditions for, the personal commitments of teachers or children.

We recognise that there is a genuine problem about the way in which R.E. teachers may make their contribution to the personal and social development of children. At face value the implications of the subject title 'Religious Education' appear to be both contradictory and undesirable. Unease about these implications is often exacerbated in the minds of some parents and teachers by their own experiences of R.E. when they were at school.

Criticisms of R.E. usually focus on the interpretations that are to be placed on 'Religious' and 'Education', and may come from opposite directions – some feeling that anything to do with religion undermines education and others holding that education undermines what religion is all about. In this manual we take the view that an equal emphasis can be placed on both – 'religious' in that we are dealing with an understanding of religion in its widest sense, and 'education' in that the exercise takes place in an educational context and conforms with educational criteria.

The first of the criticisms is really concerned with the commitments of teachers of R.E. There is an assumption that since religion is about commitment, teachers of R.E. will want to pass on their own views to children with the danger that they may indoctrinate them.

It is inevitable that teachers of R.E., like all other teachers, will have their own particular commitment to a set of beliefs and values. These commitments will differ very widely from teacher to teacher.

There is certainly no one single set of beliefs with which they will all conform; and some will not be committed to any religious tradition. It is likely however that all teachers of R.E. will have some sort of deeply held convinctions and beliefs.

It is quite clear that teachers of R.E. must not seek, either implicitly or explicitly, to indoctrinate children into their own particular outlook. At the same time they will use their professional expertise to make their views available in the classroom for children to explore in an educational context. Indeed, the teacher may well be one of the primary resources for helping children to understand the importance of commitment to beliefs and values. But teachers must tread a careful middle way between the dangers of trying to force their own views on children and the pitfalls of attempting to be so detached that children conclude that the whole exercise is academic and irrelevant.

What is certain is that without a belief in the value of the subject's aim, it will be extremely difficult to be a successful teacher of R.E. This means that teachers must be committed to the importance of being clear, thoughtful and consistent in their own set of beliefs, values and attitudes, and of encouraging children to engage in the same task.

The second criticism arises from a concern that since R.E. is an educational activity, it might actually be undermining the commitment of children who are being nurtured at home or elsewhere in a particular religious tradition. This view implies that beliefs and values which are regarded as absolute in a faith community become merely relative in the context of R.E. in schools. If R.E. does not reinforce cultural and religious norms – so the argument runs – it cannot have any value.

In an educational context the absolute status of beliefs and values for those who hold them is both recognised and respected. Far from undermining children's commitments, R.E. should help them to think more clearly and deeply about them. At the same time, there is no question of assuming that one expression of commitment has greater universal validity than another. Children will certainly be encouraged to see their own commitment in the light of other people's commitments, but with a view to mutual respect rather than mutual destruction. They will also without doubt learn from and reflect on the views of others. It is not, however, the task of R.E. to determine beforehand what the outcome of their learning and reflection might be. It is the task of R.E. to ensure that children have gained some understanding of religion by the time they leave school; that they have explored something of the relationship between religious perspectives and wider human experiences; and that they have reflected for themselves on the relevance of these perspectives and experiences for their own beliefs, attitudes and behaviour. The success of the subject can only be measured in the long term by the extent to which the exploration and reflection are continued beyond school into adult life.

PART TWO
WHAT CAN BE TAUGHT IN R.E.?

Readers ought, at this point, to be reminded of the principle aim of Religious Education with which this manual began:

Religious Education helps children mature in relation to their **own patterns of belief and behaviour** through exploring **religious beliefs and practices** and related **human experiences.**

The most significant phrases in this aim have now been highlighted because they indicate the three main areas from which religious education in schools draws its content. These three areas can be more easily represented through the diagram of the R.E. field of enquiry, shown below.

The field of enquiry provides an indication of the potential content which is suitable for use in R.E. in schools. The use of arrows in the diagram indicates that the three areas – traditional belief systems, shared human experience and individual patterns of belief – are intended to relate very closely to each other.

The first chapter in this part will concentrate on three things:

1 Explaining in more detail the three areas from which R.E. in schools draws its content.
2 Indicating some of the criteria that need to be applied when selecting from the field of enquiry topics or themes for use in the classroom.
3 Suggesting how these three areas are inter-related.

THE R.E. FIELD OF ENQUIRY

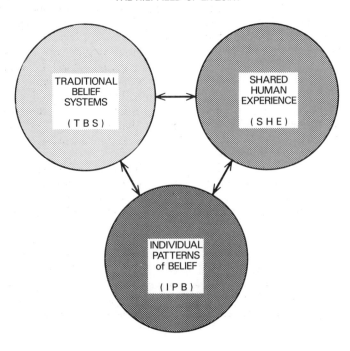

TRADITIONAL
BELIEF
SYSTEMS

(T B S)

SHARED
HUMAN
EXPERIENCE

(S H E)

INDIVIDUAL
PATTERNS
of BELIEF

(I P B)

1 The three main areas of content in R.E.

<u>TRADITIONAL BELIEF SYSTEMS</u>

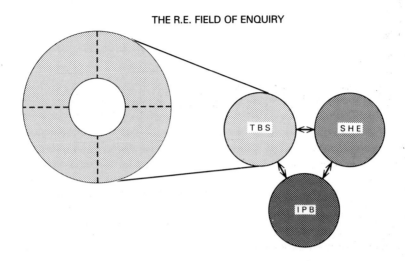

THE R.E. FIELD OF ENQUIRY

The world in which children are growing up today embraces a great variety of ideas and beliefs. Improved communications and the growth of minority groups' participation in society have made us increasingly aware of just how varied these ideas and beliefs are and how widely they range. Beliefs about the meaning and goal of life, about human nature and destiny, about what is right or wrong, about the origins of the world and the place of human beings in it – all these in one way or another influence the lives of people and the shape of cultures. With them are closely linked an equally varied range of outlooks, values, attitudes, styles of life and codes of conduct which give expression to them.

All these beliefs and ways of life are potential material for R.E. There are, however, both theoretical and practical reasons for trying to narrow down this wide field to more manageable proportions. That is why it is more appropriate in R.E. to focus attention on those beliefs and practices which are widely shared and influential in the modern world. These are the beliefs and practices which form part of coherent systems or world views, and which we refer to here as **traditional belief systems.**

At this point it is important to guard against giving false impressions. There is a sense in which the notion of a traditional belief system can be misleading. The great religions of the world are, as a rule, far from systematic and do not fit easily into categories. They are much more akin to living and moving organisms, changing and developing, responding to situations, manifest in many colours, varieties and forms. Attempts to define, analyse and dissect them into their component parts does, in one sense, destroy their living wholeness and thus their essential nature. Nevertheless, the task of education does demand that we make use of models for exploration; and, in the case of young children in particular, the sense of the vibrant whole can only be built up from a developing understanding of the constituent parts.

In using the term 'traditional belief system' we are not therefore trying to rob the reality of its living essence, but to point to the need for a suitable model that is both true to the nature of the reality and serves the educational task.

What is meant by 'systems'?
The fact that beliefs are widely shared, and hold together, however loosely, to give a kind of total response to the world, suggests that they may properly be referred to as systems. They are not, of course, rigid formulae, precisely structured or expressed in internally logical statements with inflexible codes of conduct and practice. Within these systems we undoubtedly find wide variations of interpretation, outlook and behaviour; yet each one does hold together by some common bond and

provides a distinctive world-view with which particular people and groups identify.

What is meant by 'traditional'?
Some of these systems have been more durable and pervasive than others. Some have had, and continue to have, a considerable influence over the lives of many millions of people. They form part of the rich heritage of ideas and sources of inspiration which shape great cultures. We therefore refer to them as traditional. Again, this is not to imply that they are merely museum pieces of historical interest, part of a bygone age, but that their influence has not been ephemeral, a mere passing shadow. Not only do they have a history of their own; they also continue to inspire and to command the commitment of people today. Their influence is living and vibrant.

What is meant by 'belief'?
We also refer to them as belief systems. This suggests that, from one point of view at least, they encompass a coherent view and focus upon a distinctive interpretation of life and of the world we live in. It does not, of course, imply that the only way in which these systems may be viewed is as a vehicle for providing clearly defined beliefs. Nor does it mean that there are not many other aspects which adherents may see as equally – or more – important. It is simply to recognise the way in which shared beliefs do influence and inform a range of attitudes and practice and provide a recognisable point of focus and indentity, particularly for teaching purposes.

'Belief systems' or 'religions'?
The use of the term 'belief systems' rather than 'religions' is to ensure that reference is made to other views of life which do not necessarily include a theistic or transcendent perspective. The Theravada school of Buddhism and some strands of Hinduism are of this kind. Likewise certain secular humanist philosophies, whilst not to be defined as religions, certainly embody coherent systems of belief, identifiable practices and recognisable codes of conduct.

The six major religions in Britain
For the purposes of this manual most of the examples used are drawn from the great religious traditions of the world. Reference is usually made to six major religions or traditional belief systems as providing the best illustrations and examples for R.E.

It is evident that there is a very great difficulty in trying to give a description of each of these religions. Volumes have been written about them. Where does one begin to answer a question like 'What is Christianity?' or 'What is Hinduism?' – especially bearing in mind that we are concerned with children in a classroom? It will not do to take the answer of any one individual adherent, since that person's perspective is likely to be limited and reflect the views of a particular group. Nor is a theological or philosophical perspective much use. To distill Radhakrishnan's *Ten Principal Upanishads* or Barth's *Church Dogmatics*, even down to their most basic essentials, will not help anyone to comprehend in a complete and sufficient way the variety implied in 'Hinduism' and 'Christianity'.

There are other perspectives which have provided a more analytical approach to understanding particular belief systems. A traditional approach has been to use the perspective of history, but this can appear both arid and irrelevant unless one has some prior understanding of the living reality of the system today. A more contemporary approach is provided by the so-called 'six dimensions of religion'. This, however, still remains essentially an analytical, rather than a pedagogical, model.

In seeking to answer questions such as 'What is Christianity?' and 'What is Hinduism?' we have to make use of a more practical perspective, and one which at the same time accords with the way in which a child may begin to understand a particular tradition. In other words, it is necessary to provide a model which will make some sense of the tradition, in much the same way as other subjects in the school curriculum provide models for exploring other aspects of life.

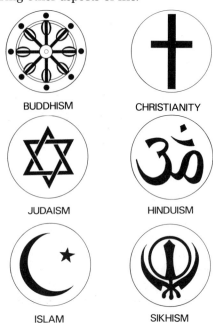

BUDDHISM CHRISTIANITY

JUDAISM HINDUISM

ISLAM SIKHISM

A model for making sense of a traditional belief system

In R.E. children are encouraged to explore belief systems as they are encountered and expressed in the world around them. In this sense the content of their R.E. lessons has a practical and contemporary orientation. What children see and hear of religion in the community or on television, and what religious people do or say, are all areas of study. Observing these external features of religion is, however, only one part of making sense of a traditional belief system.

Behind all the **observable features** can be found an inner core of beliefs, values and attitudes which are hidden and cannot be observed. This inner core of **hidden features** is also an important aspect for study. The following diagram and explanation provides the model for exploring a traditional belief system in R.E.

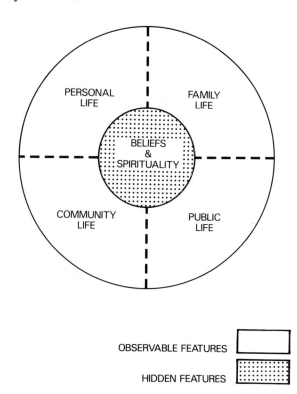

OBSERVABLE FEATURES

HIDDEN FEATURES

Observable features

Adherents of religious traditions engage in a wide range of activities which they associate with their particular faith. At first sight, all this activity may appear confusing. People celebrate festivals, bury their dead, meet in special places, say prayers, sing, march in public demonstrations, eat special foods, meditate and do a thousand and one other things.

None of these activities in itself may be particularly unusual. What will be distinctive about them is the way in which they are performed, the context where they take place, and the meaning that is given to them. In observing these activities, therefore, it is important to look for particular aspects in order to develop an understanding of their meaning and significance. The following three are particularly important.

Symbol
Observe carefully the way in which particular places are used, the way in which they are set apart, designed and furnished for particular occasions. Notice the artefacts that are used, the way in which drama and movement may express meaning, they way in which art or music may help to convey atmosphere. All these elements invite deeper exploration of the meaning and importance that may be attached to them. The liturgy of the Orthodox churches is rich in symbol, art and drama and breathes an atmosphere of reverence, awe and wonder.

Story
Many activities (though not all, by any means) are associated with a particular story or tradition. This is often an important aspect in linking the activity with the wider concerns or traditions of the religion. At the festival of Wesak, celebrating the birth, enlightenment and death of the Buddha, it is customary for stories from the life of Siddhartha Gautama to be retold.

People
Observe those who are participating in the activities, and especially the role they play. Some will be in positions of leadership and will be the focus of attention; others will be assisting or simply participating. At a traditional Hindu funeral, we may observe the role played by the eldest son, indicating the family basis of the ritual, as well as the presence of priests and other officiants who represent the wider tradition of belief and practice.

The reason why these aspects are particularly important is that they point beyond themselves to the special meaning and significance that is attached to them. At the same time they provide a 'way in' to an exploration of religious traditions, and one that is particularly suitable at primary level.

In making these observations, we need also to be careful to explore the contexts in which the activities take place. Our diagram reminds us of the **four contexts** through which an exploration of a traditional belief system can be made.

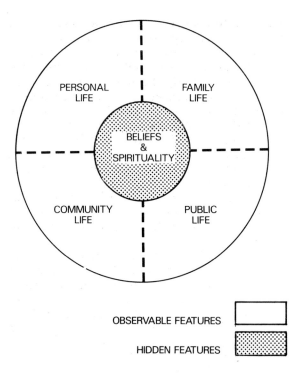

OBSERVABLE FEATURES

HIDDEN FEATURES

Public life
All religious traditions impinge in some way on wider aspects of society. Here it is important to observe the ways in which religious communities address themselves to issues in society and proclaim and uphold their beliefs in public. We are certainly familiar with the many groups who, in the name of their religion, wish to influence society in relation to such issues as abortion, capital punishment, nuclear weapons or pornography.

In exploring these observable aspects and contexts, it is also important to try to explore something of the feelings and experience of the participants. Emotions of joy and solemnity, awe and wonder, calm and excitement, serenity and sadness are often to be seen in those who are caught up in giving expression to their religion.

The exploration with which we are concerned in R.E., however, does not end at a mere observation of external features. These features are a means to an end. Since children will generally encounter religions in the first place by observing these external features, they have their place. But the purpose of the exercise is essentially to explore the meaning that is given to the activities. With this in mind we now turn to the inner part of the circle in our diagram to identify those features of a traditional belief system which are not easily observable.

Hidden features
At the heart of traditional belief systems, behind all their external features, can be found the inner core of faith, values and attitudes. Two main aspects of this inner core are particularly relevant for the purposes of R.E. – beliefs and spirituality.

Beliefs
These, of course, may be stated at different levels. Many of the beliefs to which people give expression are derived from or subsidiary to other beliefs. In this area, we are drawing attention to those beliefs which are essential to a particular tradition. In spite of differences of interpretation, they are shared by most adherents. Christian belief in Jesus Christ as the Son of God is of this kind. It is a fundamental belief, shared by all Christians, though there are varieties of interpretation among Christians as to what precisely the belief means, and there are many divisions of opinion as to what should be the appropriate way of expressing or responding to it.

The beliefs in question may not be precisely defined in any way as, for example, in a creed. They may be a general set of ideas on the basis of

Personal life
Religious behaviour is sometimes expressed in a very personal way. It is important to observe the way in which people act and express themselves as individuals. These activities may be rather different from other actions which are performed in the company of others. Prayer or meditation in most traditions expresses the most obvious form of religious practice of individuals.

Family life
Some religious activities are performed in the context of the family group and may be located in the home. In this case it is the actions of the family as a whole which we are observing. In a Jewish family, the observance of dietary rules is normally considered to be particularly important and the family context of many festivals and observances is seen as a key factor in maintaining and handing on Jewish traditions.

Community life
This is the likely context of many of the most significant activities of a religious tradition. Many (but certainly not all) religions express their ideas in activities which take place when the community of the faithful gather together. Although a Muslim may pray anywhere, either alone or in the family context, the gathering of Muslims for Jum'a prayers in the mosque on Fridays holds a special place in the life of the community.

which groups of adherents express varying views and interpretations. The way in which they are expressed will reflect different emphases. Their importance in relation to other beliefs may vary. There is therefore no attempt to organise beliefs in any kind of hierarchy. The important thing is that they are all linked together, and, taken together, they express a distinctive world-view.

In some traditions, the absence of any credal formulation is important since the essence of that tradition is not represented by adhering to propositions of belief stated verbally, but by embracing a whole way of life and social structure. Nevertheless, it is still true to say that underlying that way of life there will be certain ideas which give it shape and meaning and which are important to its identity. We have to speak in this much more tentative way when we use the word 'beliefs' in connection with the Hindu tradition. Hinduism does not have the kind of preoccupation with propositional belief which is found in some Western traditions. It would still be true to say that ideas like karma and samsara are very influential and pervasive, however ill-defined they may appear.

Spirituality

This term is used in a broad sense to include other aspects of the inner life of a tradition. The following are examples.

Values

All traditions express the outcome of their beliefs or inner life in terms of some basic ethical principles. These principles are derived from the inner life, and embody the basis on which individuals, families and communities live in relation to each other and to those outside the tradition. The lifestyle which people embrace may, to a greater or lesser degree, express these important values. In most traditions there is one key value which all the others are intended to express. In Islam, Jihad expresses a key notion of both spirituality and practice, just as love represents the key to Christian spirituality and ethical values.

Formative experiences

Those who belong to a tradition will, like all human beings, find themselves caught up in the web of emotion and feelings. Since this aspect of life is not easy to control, we may assume that within any tradition the whole range of emotions and experiences may be found. Nevertheless, all the traditions point to certain key or formative experiences which actually give shape to the tradition. In many cases particular rituals are so structured that they are designed to reproduce or relive these key experiences in the lives of participants. In some traditions we find rituals which are expressly designed to perpetuate an ancient, historical experience as a living reality in the modern community. As such, it is an essential part of that tradition's spirituality. Various rituals and practices in the Hindu and Buddhist traditions are designed to encourage and promote attitudes and experiences which express the ideal of non-attachment. In the Muslim tradition, during the important fast of Ramadan, believers recall the unique moment of revelation of the Qur'an on the Night of Power and, as it were, relive the experience.

In the Christian tradition, the sharing of the Last Supper by Jesus with his disciples just before his death is a key formative experience in the shaping of the tradition. Sharing in the sacramental rituals which arose from this experience provides for many Christians the normal means of spiritual activity and enrichment.

Random experiences

Most traditions embrace experiences which reflect the past events which were crucial to the formation of their beliefs and spirituality. On the other hand, their adherents often tell of deep spiritual experiences which occur outside the normal religious life. These occur in a random way and often in unintended forms.

Many people, for example, whether they have formal links with a religious tradition or not, believe that they have been surrounded by a presence or a power which is beyond themselves and perhaps of a supernatural kind. These feelings may be evoked by a wide range of experiences and may occur in the most unlikely ways and places. Examples of these may include a sense of calming during an otherwise traumatic experience, an awareness of a leading in a direction not previously considered, a sense of companionship or even exhilaration in times of loneliness. People who do belong to a particular religious tradition usually interpret such feelings by reference to the belief system of that tradition.

Unexplainable happenings may also be interpreted in religious terms by some people. Not uncommon among these random experiences are those which invite an appeal to a miraculous force intervening and changing what would appear to be the natural, or reasonably to be expected, outcome of a certain chain of events. All of the religious traditions cite accounts of such random and miraculous happenings.

For example, people claim to be healed by the direct intervention of God, often in the face of declared hopelessness. Others are deeply moved by a fortuitous event which changes their whole life and they attribute this to the work of some spiritual force or reality. Visions and the receiving of important revelations are also found among accounts of this kind of random spiritual experience.

When dealing with this aspect of 'hidden' qualities of traditions, it is important that at least these three understandings of the concept of spirituality are dealt with. As a general rule of thumb, they are better studied through biographical material in the primary school and in a more direct and abstract way in the secondary school.

Guidelines for dealing with traditional belief systems in the classroom

The model we have used is intended essentially to help teachers to identify the kind of material that can be used in the classroom and to give them an overview of how religious traditions might be viewed in an educational context. Here are four rules that must be followed when exploring traditional belief systems in R.E.:

1 Identify suitable topics.
2 Be aware of different perspectives within traditions.
3 Aim for an objective, fair and balanced presentation.
4 Ensure that a variety of different traditional belief systems are explored.

1 Identify suitable topics

When it comes to the question of identifying topics for R.E. from the major religious traditions, it is important that teachers pay careful regard to those areas and emphases that the tradition itself would identify as significant. Within each tradition there are a number of these key topics, but there is not usually a common theme which would link them together across all the traditions. For example, in Islam the Hajj would be such a key topic. On the other hand, the theme of 'pilgrimage' would not feature as a major topic in the exploration of Christianity.

In any R.E. programme including an exploration of Christianity we would expect to find units of work dealing with such things as baptism, Holy Communion, the Bible, Easter, the Church. These are examples of the kind of topics which would be of importance to nearly all Christians, even though there will be a wide variety of expression and interpretation in relation to them. Key topics are found in all traditions. Teachers should consult the supplementary manuals, where examples of these topics are given in more detail. The model we have been using provides a focus for teachers to consider some of the aspects and contexts through which the selected topics can be explored in the classroom – at a level suitable for the age range of the children. Within particular traditions, the topics themselves will determine some of these factors. In many cases, however, it will be possible to choose from a number of different contexts and aspects. The topic of Christian baptism, for example, could be explored in a personal, family or religious community context. The different aspects of the topic could be selected according to the teacher's objectives and the age of the children.

2 Be aware of different perspectives within traditions

A second major question is concerned with the perspective through which each tradition is approached. We have indicated that it cannot be the perspective of any one believer. That perspective might convey some real understanding of what it means to be committed to a religion and way of life: but it is unlikely to be representative of the tradition as a whole. It will tend to regard as secondary – even to denigrate or disparage – the perspective of some other believers. While it is essential in R.E. that children are able to listen to, observe and explore the faith of believers, they should not limit themselves to one single perspective. They should recognise from an early stage that people differ in their perspectives. They should be encouraged to take a broad view of a tradition as a whole; that will mean, in theory at least, that the faith and outlook of anyone who claims to belong to a tradition may be explored by the children.

3 Aim for an objective, fair and balanced presentation

If we are to help children observe a tradition as a whole, it follows that the presentation we give will aim to be as objective, fair and balanced as possible. This means that due weight will need to be given to different emphases, and teachers will need to take into consideration how they achieve a balance between some of the contrasting elements set out below.

The essential and the cultural

Some of the observable features which may be explored in the classroom will be common to all those who share a tradition. The celebration of Passover within Judaism is a common essential feature. On the other hand, the way in which it is celebrated will vary, sometimes according to Sephardi or Ashkenazi traditions, and sometimes according to national traditions. The celebration of Christmas is broadly universal within the Christian Church, but many of its elements (e.g. the mid-winter setting) are culturally determined in the northern hemisphere; others vary according to national boundaries (e.g. the place given to St Nicholas in the celebrations).

The mainstream and the peripheral

In presenting any tradition, it is clearly important that children are made aware of the way in which the great majority express their faith and commitment. At the same time, since they need to appreciate different expressions and viewpoints, due regard will need to be given to some of those aspects and emphases which are represented by minorities. For example, since within the Christian tradition as a whole the Roman Catholic Church represents the majority of Christians, some knowledge and appreciation of Roman Catholicism and its emphases is basic to an understanding of the tradition as a whole. Quakers, on the other hand, are numerically a very minor and peripheral group. Nevertheless, an understanding of their tradition is also important since it provides a contrast of interpretation and practice. We could say the same about the Sufi tradition in Islam, or the Hasidim in Judaism.

The local and the global

The basis for the exploration of a religious tradition will, in many cases, be found within a local community. Where possible, it is highly desirable that children should have first-hand access to a living and local expression of faith. This should not, however, form their total perspective, since it could as a result be distorted in a number of ways. This applies particularly to those religious groups which have settled in the United Kingdom relatively recently, and who have been acutely aware of the need both to preserve their distinctiveness and to conform with local dictates. For example, the way in which Sikh and Hindu groups tend to meet regularly and congregationally on Sunday is dictated by local conditions and would not be representative of Sikhism or Hinduism in India. Moreover, the way in which particular groups practise their faith may not be wholly typical. For example, the celebrations of Diwali in the United Kingdom are drawn mainly from northern Indian traditions, and are less typical of southern Indians, who are in a small minority in Britain.

The popular and the intellectual

A tension has always existed between the great mass of practitioners and those teachers and exponents who have absorbed their tradition at the philosophical level. Popular forms of art, music or devotion may appear crude and unsophisticated to a guru or theologian. This dichotomy is well illustrated in the way different groups describe or conceptualise God, ranging from very mundane and concrete images to highly abstract concepts. At a practical level it may be observed in the different attitudes found within the Hindu tradition, in which the deities represented in popular images are regarded by other Hindus as useful but inessential aids to the practice of devotion. We may observe the same tendency in traditions which place much greater emphasis on the verbal expression of religion, some insisting on the literal truth of what is written, and others insisting on the need to interpret verbal images in a more sophisticated way. In R.E. it is important that children explore the popular dimension since it is the one which they are initially most likely to encounter. At the same time, they should gradually appreciate more sophisticated expressions of the same tradition.

The traditional and the radical

These two are closely related to the popular and intellectual interpretations, but are not identical with them. They are found especially in relation to two areas. The first is the cultic area, where traditionalists seek to maintain the form of a tradition in contrast to the radicals who seek to keep alive the spirit of a tradition – in some cases with little regard for the traditional form. The second is the ethical area, where traditionalists will tend to hold on to a literal interpretation of traditional codes and to apply them literally to contemporary situations: radicals, on the other hand, tend to apply traditional codes to contemporary situations by seeking to interpret the spirit of the code in the light of new considerations and changing circumstances. A similar pattern is found in the contrast between those who view their own tradition as uniquely authentic and adopt an exclusive attitude to those who do not share it; and those, on the other hand, who see their own tradition in a more relative way, and are prepared to adopt a more open or inclusive attitude to unbelievers or those of another persuasion. Significant examples of this contrast are most apparent when considering some contemporary moral issues. At a later stage in their schooling children should be developing an awareness of the different approaches to issues represented by these contrasting attitudes.

4   Ensure that a variety of traditional belief systems are explored

This leads to the last question, that of achieving an overall balance in exploring religious traditions within a 5 – 16 R.E. programme. The six major religious traditions will certainly feature in the total programme, but it is not necessary, for the purpose of a balanced R.E. programme, that children should explore all six in equal measure. In the total programme, the criteria for balance are that by the age of sixteen children should:

(a) have a basic understanding, and be able to recognise, the main features of the six traditions;
(b) have considered non-religious ideas and ideals;
(c) have developed a deeper understanding of at least two and no more than three of the six traditions; one of these should be the Christian tradition;
(d) have had the opportunity, as far as possible, to explore their own particular tradition in an educational context.

These criteria are intended to provide a balance of breadth and depth in the exploration of religious traditions. To attempt to cover all six equally would be to over-emphasise breadth at the expense of depth, and would tend towards superficiality. To deal with only one tradition would fail to satisfy the criterion of breadth, and would certainly not lead to a balanced understanding of the diversity of religion.

In conclusion, however, it must be emphasised that the exploring of religious traditions is only one part of R.E. An over-emphasis on traditional belief systems at the expense of other areas of the field of enquiry will lead to an unbalanced Religious Education and will frustrate the achievement of the subject's aim.

SHARED HUMAN EXPERIENCE

The term used to describe this second area of the field of enquiry in R.E. is at first sight unhelpfully vague. Human experience can cover absolutely anything and there is a sense in which any human experience may be useful for consideration in R.E. In the sense intended here, however, we are looking at a more limited range of experiences.

What is meant by shared human experience?

In the first place, we are concerned with experiences which are widely shared. We are not looking at the unique experiences of millions of isolated individuals but at the kind of experiences which fall to all, or at least most, human beings. In the second place, we are looking at experiences which are not the preserve of any one group of people, but at those which are typical of human beings simply by virtue of their common human bond. In the third place we are concerned with particularly significant experiences. For our purposes, the experiences which are regarded as significant are those which have prompted, and continue to prompt, the puzzling or ultimate questions about life, to which there appear to be no final answers. It is these questions which lend importance to the experiences. Once again, we use the same basic design for a diagram which helps to make sense of the kind of aspects we are concerned with in this area of R.E. As part of the R.E. field of

SHARED HUMAN EXPERIENCE

THE R.E. FIELD OF ENQUIRY

A model for making sense of shared human experience

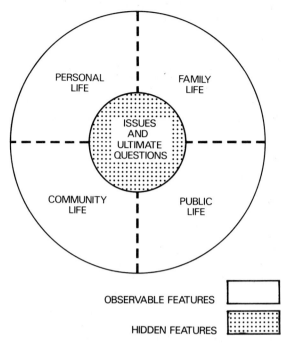

OBSERVABLE FEATURES

HIDDEN FEATURES

enquiry, the shared human experience circle provides a means of identifying potential content which can be made available for exploration in the classroom.

An exploration of shared human experience is again an exploration of observable and hidden features. There is observable behaviour, represented by the outer circle, and questions about human life and experience, represented by the inner core. It is the latter which give significance to the former. It may, therefore, be more useful in this case to begin by referring to these hidden features.

Hidden features

Ultimate questions
It is by no means easy to give a clear definition of ultimate questions. They are sometimes referred to as unanswerable questions – but are these questions unanswerable because of our lack of sufficient knowledge, or because, as some assert, they are meaningless? Moreover, although there is a sense in which they are unanswerable, it is curious how human beings are forever answering them. They are not, of course, answering them with verifiable statements of fact. If they are wise, they will always preface their answers with such words as 'I/we believe...' for these questions can only be answered by an expression of belief, a statement of faith.

Whether the questions appear to be meaningless or not, they are certainly those which have engaged the sharpest minds and stirred the deepest emotions. The answers that are given are fundamental to all outlooks on life, non-religious or religious. Not everyone, by any means, asks these questions all the time, or in the same form, or with the same force or urgency: yet they have a habit of recurring and seem inescapable. They are ultimate questions in the sense that they ask about ultimate things – questions beyond which there are no more questions; questions 'at the end of the line'.

It may be helpful if we identify these questions as being concerned with a number of general areas of human experience, as represented in this diagram:

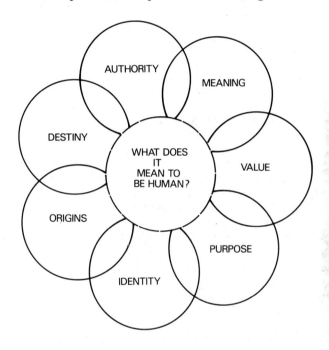

All these general areas are interrelated with the ultimate question 'What does it mean to be human?' The answer we give to that question will normally define and shape the answers we give to the other questions – or vice versa. Those who believe that human beings are the end product of a long chain of random selection, or the byproducts of an ongoing historical process, or eternal and immaterial souls confined in a temporal and material body, or the children of a loving and compassionate God, will all have widely differing perspectives when it comes to looking at the other questions.

Each of these general areas gives rise to a number of more detailed questions, which have

TABLE 1 Ultimate questions	
GENERAL AREA	EXAMPLE QUESTIONS
Authority	Why should I do as you say? Is there a God? Who says I shouldn't steal?
Meaning	Why do the innocent suffer? Where is happiness to be found? What is truth?
Value	What is most important to me? Do people matter more than things? Why don't we care?
Purpose	What is life for? What is success? What should my ambition be?
Identity	Who am I? Who do I belong to? Why are we different?
Origins	Why did the world begin? Where is the source of life to be found? When does life start?
Destiny	Is there life after death? What future is there for us? What will become of me?

this ultimate dimension to them. The questions may be very general, or they may be couched in more personal terms. Those which are given in Table 1 (opposite) as examples – and there are many more – are not by any means confined to just one of the general areas we have identified. They overlap very considerably.

Issues and experiences
Underlying the ultimate questions and often giving rise to them, is a wide range of issues and experiences. This is because the questions themselves have an important existential and emotional dimension to them. They are not merely the ramblings of abstract thinkers. The reasons why the questions are so important and so persistent is that they arise out of some of our deepest emotions and our most compelling experiences. The feelings and experiences are closely interwoven, and we are unwise to try to distinguish too sharply between them.

The kind of experiences to which we refer are those which often come to the surface in crisis situations – when people are confronted with difficult decisions, or faced with impossible circumstances, or overwhelmed by insoluble problems. The pain of suffering ('Why should this happen to me?') or the approach of death ('Is there any future?'): deciding about the future, whether one's own or another's ('Should I have an abortion?'); or trying to find solutions to seemingly intractable problems of personal and social relationships ('Should I get married?', 'How should we combat racism?'); these are all pressing situations which force upon us questions of purpose or meaning, authority or identity. Feelings of fear or doubt, guilt or helplessness may amplify the problem and make a solution even more pressing.

There are other experiences which come to people in unexpected ways – experiences which heighten the emotions and sometimes open up questions not usually considered before. Experiences of awe, wonder, mystery or beauty are of this kind. They may come to people when they suddenly become aware of the powerful forces of nature or when they hold a newborn child, and they may inspire feelings of fear, joy or devotion.

There are feelings, too, which derive from an ongoing awareness of human finiteness and the uncertainty of life, or from a sense of responsibility for the world we live in and those around us. At the same time, we should not confine ourselves just to those feelings and experiences which appear to be problematic, or serious, or negative or morbid. Many of the important questions of life come to

light through experiences of great joyfulness, celebration and ecstasy; and human beings have a great capacity for responding in positive ways to the difficulties and hardships of life.

It is not surprising, therefore, that the kind of feelings we are concerned with here are found in pairs of opposites – joy and sorrow, certainty and doubt, belonging and loneliness, hope and despair, love and hate. They represent the great range of emotions through which people express themselves, and through which they respond both to the unexpected and the inevitable.

Observable features
Ultimate questions and underlying feelings and responses are, however, intangible. They only become evident through the observable behaviour that people use to express themselves in particular situations. The diagram we have used once again focusses on four contexts in which this observable behaviour can be explored:

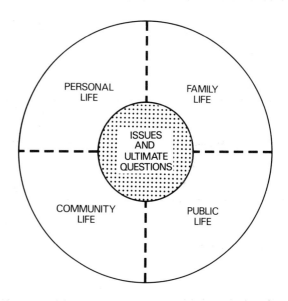

This focus on contexts reminds us of the kind of situations it will be useful to explore in R.E. in order to sharpen children's understanding of the issues and ultimate questions that arise from them. All four contexts – personal life, family life, community life and public life – are important in order that a balanced approach may be achieved. Once again an excessive concentration on individual behaviour, for example, may fail to raise issues quite as sharply as they could be raised by exploring situations in other contexts.

When we were dealing with traditional belief systems, we found that examples of observable behaviour could be identified and described with relative ease – celebrating festivals, performing rituals, meeting in buildings and so on. With the use of suitable resources these can all be brought into the classroom for children to explore.

This exercise is less easy with regard to shared human experience where any human behaviour or situation could be used as a basis for exploration, and where, on the whole, it is impossible to specify in advance the particular behaviours and situations which might serve as illustrations. Of course, specific religious activities can (and should) themselves be used as illustrations, since they are part of human experience.

In R.E., the guiding principle in identifying an appropriate behaviour or situation must always be that it has the greatest potential for raising ultimate questions and for exploring the issues and experiences that underlie them.

Guidelines for identifying suitable classroom topics which are good examples of shared human experience

While it is not so easy to identify quickly the kind of topics or situations which best serve this exploration of shared human experience, it is possible to suggest the sort of categories or themes which offer a potential wealth of suitable material.

The general categories identified in Table 2 provide an indication of the sorts of specific topics and situations which might provide good examples for R.E. of aspects of shared human experience. Teachers will be aware of other suitable categories, and will be able to draw on their own knowledge and experiences in choosing the best examples.

The examples in Tables 3 and 4 (pages 22–3) illustrate the way in which specific topics can be drawn from the four contexts and from the general categories (see Table 2), and how they open up the way for exploring feelings and experiences and some of the ultimate questions which may underlie them. For the sake of clarity, four examples are given of topics which might be more suitable for the primary school (Table 3), and four for the secondary school (Table 4).

When identifying suitable classroom topics it might also be useful to recognise that:

(a) many of the shared human experience topics are likely to be explored from different perspectives in other areas of the curriculum. Careful liaison between teachers and departments is essential;

(b) the distinctive perspective of R.E. should be carefully preserved when a topic crosses subject boundaries;

(c) the essential value of dealing with shared human experience topics in R.E. lies in their potential for raising ultimate questions and exploring a variety of possible answers.

TABLE 2 General categories and potential areas for exploring shared human experiences

CATEGORIES OF HUMAN EXPERIENCE	POTENTIAL AREAS FOR IDENTIFYING TOPICS
The natural world	Human awareness of the world about us – the orderliness of nature, regularity of seasons, resources for food, energy and wealth; the awe-inspiring aspects, natural wonders and disasters, power of natural forces; the interrelatedness of all living things; the vastness of the universe and the details of the microcosm; the origins and future of the earth; the natural life cycle.
Relationships	Relationships of friendship and enmity, both personal and social; the family and relationships within the family; belonging to groups based on interest, cause or belief; relationships of equality, superiority or inferiority; personal, familial, social and national identity.
Rules and issues	The rules by which people live; codes of behaviour; legal and moral rules; personal and social moral issues, such as war and peace, inequality, human rights, poverty and affluence, law and order, euthanasia and abortion, the environment, democracy.
Stages of life	The human life process and the changes in outlook that growth and decay bring; experiences associated with childbirth, maturation, old age and death; rites of passage, particularly those associated with birth, initiation, marriage and death.
Celebrations	Ceremonies which mark important occasions in personal and community life; birthdays, anniversaries, festivals, fasts and solemn days; community, national and religious occasions; celebrations of events, people and values.
Lifestyles	The way of living that people adopt as an expression of their idenity, belief or culture; customs of food and clothing; communal, regimented and independent lifestyles, monastic and ascetic patterns of living; competitive and cooperative lifestyles, lifestyles which represent a non-conformist reaction to current norms e.g. vegetarianism.
Suffering	Human suffering as a result of disease, natural disasters, accidents; suffering as a result of war, violence and other conflict; cruelty to other human beings and animals; persecution, racial discrimination, and oppression in any form; the Holocaust; human responses to the problems of evil and suffering.

TABLE 3 **Specific topics drawn from the four contexts of shared human experience – Primary examples**

	EXAMPLE SITUATION/ TOPIC	EXPLORING FEELINGS AND EXPERIENCES OF...	RAISING THE ULTIMATE QUESTIONS...
1. Personal life (relationships)	**Myself – what I love** Some of the things (and people) who give me pleasure – things I have, things I do, people I like best.	pleasure happiness excitement contentment	Do people matter more than things? What is most valuable to me?
2. Family life (stages of life)	**The Jones's new baby** The parents' excitement at having a new life to share. How they look after the baby. Other members of the family share their joy. They think about things they need to do and perhaps about how their child will grow up.	care and protection wonder and mystery happiness hopefulness	What is love? What does the future hold?
3. Community life (natural world)	**Explaining how the world began** Looking at a number of stories told in different communities around the world to explain its origin and purpose – particularly the place of human beings.	awe and wonder uncertainty mystery fear	How did it all begin? Who am I?
4. Public life (relationships)	**The human family** Exploring some of the differences between groups of people – and the things all people have in common.	friendliness belonging fear/embarrassment	What makes us human? Why are we different?

	EXAMPLE SITUATION/TOPIC	EXPLORING FEELINGS AND EXPERIENCES OF...	RAISING THE ULTIMATE QUESTIONS...
1. Personal life (rules and issues)	Private Schultz was a World War II soldier. He took part in a raid on a village, and was afterwards ordered by his commander to join a firing squad to execute all the men of the village. He refused and, in spite of pleas and remonstrations, continued to do so. He was ordered to line up with the villagers. Removing his military insignia, he stood linking hands with the villagers and was shot with them.	Fear in the face of death Revulsion at human brutality Confusion at a conflict of loyalties	Is my conscience the best guide? Which is more important – my life or what is right? What is our true identity?
2. Family life (celebrations)	Mr and Mrs Smith are celebrating their golden wedding with their family and a wide circle of friends. The couple are retired, and are able to look back on a long life in which they have worked hard, endured difficulties together and brought up a large family. It is an occasion for celebration and looking back with some satisfaction at their achievements together.	Contentment and satisfaction in achievement Joy in the presence of family and friends Nostalgia (in the sense of a hankering for the good old days)	Where is the greatest happiness to be found? What is success? Who is most important to me?
3. Community life (stages of life)	Initiation ceremonies are a traditional way of marking an important stage when people become clearly identified with a particular group or community. A number of examples – being confirmed, becoming bar Mitzvah or joining the Scouts – serve as illustrations of the way in which people highlight the importance of the group and its values.	Determination to fulfil one's vows Belonging to a group Anticipation at a new beginning, etc.	Who am I? What should I be aiming for? Why be different?
4. Public life (suffering)	A serious famine has occurred, and the outlook is bleak for the sufferers. Various voluntary agencies are appealing for emergency help. Various governments are finding it difficult to agree about what should be done and appear to be looking for political capital from the situation.	Concern for those who suffer Anger and frustration that little is done Guilt at one's own comfort Indifference	Why do the innocent suffer? Why should I care? What is a human being worth?

TABLE 4 **Specific topics drawn from the general categories (Table 2) for exploring shared human experience – Secondary examples**

INDIVIDUAL PATTERNS OF BELIEF

THE R.E. FIELD OF ENQUIRY

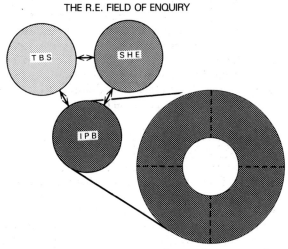

It may appear strange to single out this particular area of potential content for R.E. It is not, however, referring to individuals in a general sense, but to those individuals who find themselves participating in a particular class at a particular time – teachers as well as children. It is essential to remember in R.E. that potential content is located not only outside the classroom, but is also present in the classroom.

Why is an exploration of individual patterns of belief important in R.E.?
There are at least three good reasons why this area is important, and why it is to be distinguished from the others.

1 It is inevitable that children (and teachers) will bring into the classroom their own personal beliefs and sense of identity (however embryonic they may be), and their own attitudes and experiences. These are the materials of the subject which are closest to the children themselves and of most relevance to them. They include those experiences which are most immediate to them, as well as those which apparently assume the greatest importance for them. Because of this relevance and immediacy for individuals, particular experiences, perceptions and behaviour may be held to be not only significant, but also normative – the way I perceive things is the way everyone perceives things. That, of course, is not true, but for the purposes of R.E., it is a distinctive and important perception. R.E. is concerned to develop and broaden that perspective.

2 It is evident that the beliefs and behaviour that children bring into the classroom will have been informed and influenced by a whole range of factors. How far these influences impinge on children will vary from individual to individual. Some may have a very strong sense of identity, derived from their own family or cultural group. Others may not. The point is, however, that it is highly unlikely that any individual will conform entirely with externally imposed norms. A number of other factors will have influenced their perception. While they may conform outwardly, they do in fact in many cases see things quite differently. They may use the language handed on to them by others, but their actual understanding of what it means may be far from what is intended. It is equally true as a general principle that individual patterns of belief and behaviour rarely conform in detail with group norms.

3 Education – and, more specifically, R.E. – is not primarily concerned with children as recipients of information, suitably packaged and delivered to them, or as units to be trained or indoctrinated in cultural norms. If it were, then the perceptions and sense of identity of individuals could have no real relevance as potential content. They only assume major significance where the educational goals are directed specifically to the child's own beliefs and values and are encouraging constructive and creative thinking about these beliefs and values.

A model for making sense of individual patterns of belief
For the purpose of clarifying this third area of potential content for R.E., the same basic design for a diagram taken from the R.E. field of enquiry applies.

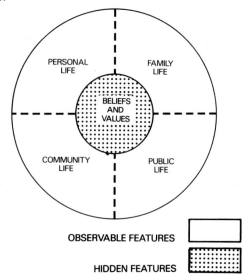

It is not necessary in this case to break down each of the parts of this diagram in detail. The observable features of individuals may once again be explored in the same four contexts. There is also a progression from behaviour through feelings and experiences to the child's own beliefs and values – the hidden features.

It is clearly impossible to define beforehand the pattern of behaviour, experience and value that each child will bring into the classroom. It will vary greatly from child to child, class to class, age to age. The essential point, however, is that this area is as important as the other two as a source of potential content for exploration in the classroom. Reference should be constantly made to this area in any teaching programme. Although it cannot be planned as part of the formal curriculum of the subject, it is of the greatest importance.

Individual patterns of belief in the classroom

The way in which individual patterns of belief emerge in the classroom, and become material for exploration, is entirely informal and ad hoc. An objection might arise in discussion; a child may point out a quite different way of looking at something; a question may be raised at the start of the lesson.'

'Miss, Tracey and I have been arguing about what happens to you when you die. What do you think?' or 'Miss, my Dad doesn't agree with that' or 'Sir, when we have Diwali, we read a different story'. The teacher of R.E. cannot of course plan ahead for these reactions and contributions. On the other hand, the sensitive teacher will always be looking for opportunities to include and develop these more personal and individual contributions in a way which may benefit the whole class.

HOW DO THE THREE AREAS OF CONTENT RELATE TO EACH OTHER?

We have so far examined three main areas as sources of content for R.E. Any programme of R.E. that fails to help children explore all three areas will in some way fail to achieve the aim of the subject. To concentrate on one area at the expense of the others will distort it. Yet the three areas are not chosen randomly nor are they identified as three distinct entities. They are closely related to each other, and this interrelationship is itself part of the essential field of enquiry of the subject.

The point is emphasised in the diagram, where the arrows draw attention to the relationships in question. They indicate the way in which each area relates to, and influences, the others.

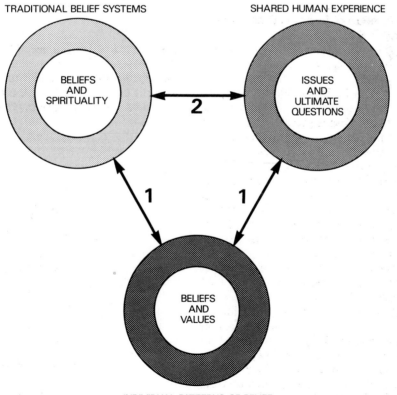

TRADITIONAL BELIEF SYSTEMS

SHARED HUMAN EXPERIENCE

BELIEFS AND SPIRITUALITY

ISSUES AND ULTIMATE QUESTIONS

2

1

1

BELIEFS AND VALUES

INDIVIDUAL PATTERNS OF BELIEF

The relationship of the individual to traditional belief systems and shared human experience

The first of these relationships (marked **1** in the diagram) is that which links individual patterns of belief – in our case those of the child and the teacher in the classroom – with shared human experience and with traditional belief systems. The arrows indicate a two-way relationship between the individual and the other two areas. This relationship can be characterised by the use of the words 'participating', 'valuing' and 'adopting'. These point to the different levels at which we all relate to the total experience, knowledge and achievements of humanity, including those enshrined in the traditional belief systems.

Participating

All people obviously participate in the general shared experience of mankind in some way or another and at one level or another. Many pupils will be aware of the big questions which life presents and they will have had experiences which highlight life's mystery and challenge, including some that suggest the possibility of transcendent realities.

Equally, all individuals participate in particular cultures. We cannot jump out of our historical and cultural skins. We are related in some way to particular traditional belief systems. They contribute to our identity and we participate in their ongoing life.

Valuing

All individuals, however, engage in a process of selection in relation to life's experiences and the traditions to which we belong. Some aspects become increasingly more valuable to us and others cease to attract our attention. The pupils' maturity in relation to their own pattern of belief and behaviour is enhanced as they discover those aspects of life which are becoming more important to them and those which have little or no value to them.

Adopting

At another level many individuals consciously go beyond a simple participation in the culturally conditioned life about them. They identify with certain groups, lifestyles and value systems and adopt a particular way of life. Certain human and/or traditional characteristics are seen not only as being important and valuable, they become the focal point of the individual's own sense of identity.

In reality, relationships between individuals and systems are rarely as simple as the above analysis suggests. Yet it is clearly possible to observe these different levels of response. It may be illustrated, for example, by the way in which Christmas is celebrated in Britain today. Some will carry on the tradition without considering its origin or religious significance. Others will attach value to what it represents in a general kind of way. Others will see it as a highlight of their own faith and commitment.

The relationship between traditional belief systems and shared human experience

The second relationship with which we are concerned (marked **2** in the diagram) is that which links traditional belief systems with shared human experience. Again the double-headed arrow suggests a two-way relationship and we use three words to describe something of the essential characteristics of this complex relationship.

Interpreting

There is a very real sense in which the traditional belief systems exist to provide a framework of understanding and way of responding to the mysteries and challenges of human life. In some cases this interpreting quality may be seen as providing answers, on the basis of faith, to ultimate questions. In others it may take the form of providing a framework in which the questions remain open and mysterious.

Supporting

There is also a kind of psychological dimension to the relationship between the belief systems and human experience. The experience of being human does not simply pose questions at an intellectual level. It also presents problems at an emotional level. In particular there are experiences which shatter confidence and undermine the fabric of life, as well as those which stimulate determination and courage. At this point the various belief systems provide, in their own ways, means for supporting those who need help and encouragement and outlets for courageous and adventurous exploits.

Challenging

Thirdly, the traditional belief systems offer important challenges to what might generally be believed, valued and done by the majority of people at a given time. Because they encapsulate ideals, visions and ultimate goals, they often have the capacity to call on people to rise above their immediate circumstances and to pursue nobler ends. They can suggest new ways of looking at things, open up new horizons and possibilities and raise new questions about life. Similarly, developments within shared human experience can and often do present challenges to the traditions to re-think, or at least re-express, some of their basic beliefs and commitments.

The R.E. field of enquiry summarised
We may now summarise the R.E. field of enquiry by referring again to the original model and indicating the relationships we have been describing. The field of enquiry sets out the potential range of content which the subject may explore. It comprises three interrelated areas. These are not separate, static bodies of knowledge, but a dynamic whole. It is from the total field of enquiry that appropriate topics may be selected for the classroom.

THE R.E. FIELD OF ENQUIRY

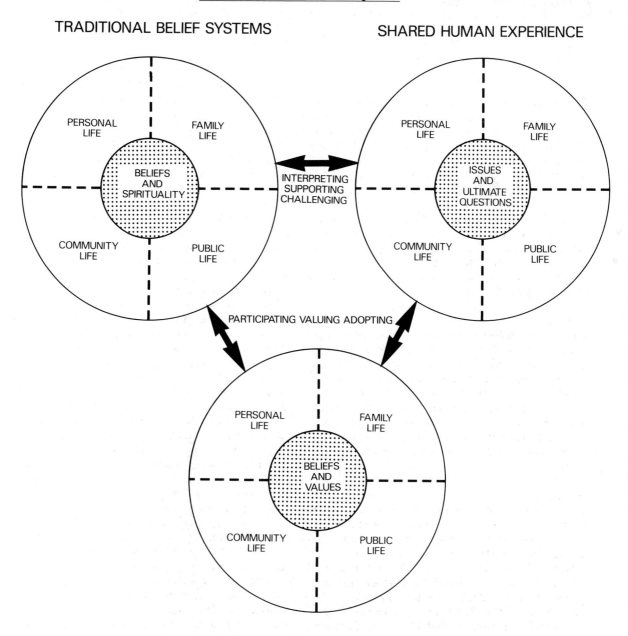

2 Concepts, skills and attitudes in R.E.

In examining the question of what can be taught in R.E. we have so far looked at the general scope of the field of enquiry, and at some basic principles of selection. We have also referred to the relationships between the three areas.

As with other subjects, the teacher of R.E. has the task of helping children to develop their understanding by encouraging them to acquire and use a range of concepts, skills and attitudes.

WHAT ARE CONCEPTS IN R.E.?

Concepts are essentially abstract ideas which help in the task of making some sort of sense and order out of a variety of information, and which contribute to the formation of models for understanding. In R.E. we are concerned with developing an understanding of the three areas of the field of enquiry and of the relationships between them.

When we were looking at the field of enquiry, we drew attention in particular to the distinction between those aspects which may be observed, and those which may be inferred. That there is a relationship between the two is obvious. It is in the exploration of this relationship that concepts are particularly important.

For example, we may observe a religious ritual in which one person (who may be easily distinguishable by dress, demeanour or position) plays a leading and directing role. Underlying this ritual, and giving significance to the leader in question, there will be a range of ideas and beliefs. To explore the relationships between what may be observed and what is hidden, concepts such as authority or the sacred may be particularly useful in building up an understanding not only of the ritual in question, but of its relationship with other rituals and people. Indeed, concepts such as these are not merely incidental to R.E.; they actually give shape to the task in which the subject is engaged. They provide a means by which children can begin to make links with other aspects of the field of enquiry, and in particular the links between the three main areas.

At this point it may be useful to begin to identify the kind of concepts with which R.E. is especially concerned. Those suggested here are in no way intended to be exhaustive. They do however help to illustrate the various levels of generality and particularity in the concepts.

Concepts within shared human experience

If we begin with the area of shared human experience, we find that the most general level of concepts are those which encompass the main categories of ultimate questions, i.e. 'authority', 'destiny', 'origins', 'meaning', 'value', 'purpose'. Beyond these there are more particular concepts which encompass aspects of the general concepts. For example, the concept of 'evolution' is one which helps to illuminate and define the more general category of 'origins'. The concept of 'creation' is, of course, another. At a further level of particularity, the concept of 'natural selection' gives more precise definition to one aspect of 'evolution'.

Concepts within traditional belief systems

Likewise, in the area of traditional belief systems, we can make use of a wide range of concepts at various levels. At the most general level, there are probably only a limited number of concepts which are not peculiar to any tradition, but which span them all. For example, the concept of 'salvation' is relevant to an understanding of all traditions, and may be the prime or key concept for understanding them. But there are others, such as 'soul', 'God', 'faith', 'the sacred', 'symbol' and 'spirituality'. We must be very careful, of course, how we use them, for they are all interpreted in subtly different ways in each of the traditions, and there is always the danger of imposing concepts on to a tradition which will not bear them. The use of the concepts 'God' or 'soul' in connection with Buddhism is quite misleading.

At a second and more specific level, we may consider some of the concepts which reflect the ideas of groups of traditions, especially those which are sometimes referred to as Western and Eastern. Concepts such as 'monotheism', 'revelation', 'love' and 'judgement' are especially important in those traditions which stem from Judaism and the concepts of 'karma', 'samsara', 'maya', and 'non-attachment' belong within the traditions emanating from Hinduism. At the third level are those concepts which belong within particular traditons and which, not surprisingly, are closely related to their key beliefs and values. Concepts such as 'sacrament', 'image', 'kosher' and 'anicca' are of this kind.

It is perhaps important to note here that any appreciation of traditional belief systems will involve children in acquiring and using a range of technical terms. These terms are essentially descriptive, rather than conceptual. Words such as gurdwara, priest, Qur'an and sangha enable children to make clear identifications and to be accurate in their descriptions. There will, of course, be points where some of the technical terms used are also concepts. For the purposes of identification at this stage it would be pedantic to draw up hard and fast rules for distinguishing between the uses. This distinction may, however, be useful when it comes to the processes by which children acquire abstract concepts.

HOW ARE CONCEPTS ACQUIRED IN R.E.?

Although we deal in more detail later with the way in which children's understanding develops in R.E., it is essential that we make it clear at this point that the concepts we are considering are part of the 'ends' rather than the 'means' of R.E. There is no suggestion that these abstract concepts are the basic diet of the infant or primary school. An understanding of them will, however, help primary teachers to be aware of the kind of direction in which they are moving and of the ways in which they can prepare the ground for their children to acquire and use them.

While we have looked at different levels of particularity, we have not been suggesting that there is any kind of hierarchy of concepts which children may be able to use from a relatively early age. They will undoubtedly in due course refine their understanding of them. It would be very unusual in R.E. if primary children did not use the word God. On the other hand, the concept of 'Trinity' is much too sophisticated for primary children to handle in any meaningful way. The important thing about most of the concepts used in R.E. is that they are imprecise and open to different interpretations, and teachers need to help children to go on exploring them, rather than suggesting that there is an acceptable and all-inclusive definition of them.

In recognising that primary – and many secondary – children will not be able to use some of the abstract concepts, teachers can still lay the foundations on which they can build their ideas. The principle is that children will build up abstract concepts from concrete examples. Thus, in the primary school, they will not be tackling the concept of 'spirituality', but they may be looking at those aspects of a person's life which indicate or point towards 'what makes them tick'. They may not be considering the concept of 'ahimsa' but they may be reading the story of Gandhi's life and thus preparing the way for understanding the concept.

This is where some of the technical terms we discussed earlier may be useful in building concepts. Words such as kosher are both descriptive (children can learn the foods that are so described) and conceptual (they can later begin to appreciate why the concept of 'kosher' is important for Jewish people).

The same principle applies in relation to the concepts of shared human experience. It would be ridiculous to suggest that infants will be considering the concepts of 'evolution' or 'creation'. On the other hand, when very young children express curiosity about where things come from or how they began in the first place they are beginning an exploration that will go on for many years.

WHAT ARE THE SKILLS AND ATTITUDES THAT SHOULD BE DEVELOPED IN R.E.?

The aim of the subject is achieved through the interaction of children with their teacher and with the R.E. field of enquiry. This interaction is only effectively brought about when children acquire the necessary abilities and skills to make it work, and when they develop certain basic attitudes that are essential to their learning.

It would be a mistake to suggest that R.E. is simply 'skills-based' – that the acquisition of certain basic knowledge is of secondary or minor importance. That would be to claim much too high a status for the skills and attitudes listed here in relation to the subject. It would, moreover, suggest that the subject has, by its nature, a range of skills which distinguish it from any other area of the curriculum. It is very doubtful whether this is so, or whether a case for such a view could be made out.

R.E. does, however, require the development of particular skills and attitudes, and these are set out below under five headings.

Skills of investigation and enquiry
As with other subjects, children learning R.E. need to develop the skills of acquiring knowledge. At a basic level, this will include observing, recording and classifying information about subject matter explored in the classroom and elsewhere. Children need to be encouraged to raise questions about what they are observing so that they are not merely gathering information and describing what they see, but are also developing their understanding.

This is an exercise in which the teacher has a most important role to play. Prompting the right kind of questions will help to develop understanding as well as curiosity. It is an area in which primary teachers, with their clear emphasis on working with individuals and groups, are particularly adept. In Religious Education many of the things which children study will have hidden significance which is not always clear to the untrained observer. Teachers will want to encourage children to look for the meaning behind what they see, and not to assume a literal interpretation. For example, when observing religious behaviour, children need to be encouraged to ask questions about why people behave the way they do, what meaning is attached to their actions, what feelings and experiences might be involved for them, and what beliefs and ideas they might be expressing. When looking more generally at human experiences, children can be encouraged to ask what questions of a more general nature are raised by the experience they are observing.

In R.E. one of the best ways of helping children to explore is to present them with situations where they encounter what they are studying at first hand. Where possible they should be able to witness religious behaviour and participate in situations which embody general human experiences. Meeting members of various faith communities either in their homes or places of worship, or in school, for example, is one of the best ways of ensuring that children have first-hand experiences of what they are studying. In this situation, however, they need to develop the kind of skills that help them to discern the difference between expressions of belief and statements of fact, or to recognise what they are seeing as particular expressions which may not be universal.

As children mature they should have developed those more sophisticated skills which can discern, for example, the difference between a balanced presentation and what is propaganda or advertisement. In listening to those who speak from the standpoint of faith (whether religious or non-religious) the skills of recognising these different styles of discourse are of the greatest importance for children's maturation.

Social and interactive skills

Since R.E. is primarily concerned with the personal and social development of children, it follows that relationship skills are central to the nature and aims of the subject (as of any educational programme). They are not merely means to an end. Learning about and learning from people who are different from ourselves is of the essence of R.E. To achieve this learning, children must be able to relate to their peers, and to older adults, and express their own commitments and convictions in an atmosphere of open enquiry, mutual respect and tolerance.

Respect for the views of others in the class is essential if children are to learn from each other. This does not mean encouraging children to show a bland acceptance of anyone else's ideas, but at least to recognise how important ideas are for those who hold them strongly. It also means recognising the limitations of one's own ideas and the struggle in which all are engaged to think and act consistently.

Tolerance, together with respect, is absolutely central to any educational enterprise. There has to be a point where people agree to differ without entering into conflict and aggression – or without disdaining and disregarding others. Since R.E. is a subject in which controversy is inevitable, the teacher has an important role to play in making sure that it is used creatively and not destructively.

Probably the most important skill that the R.E. teacher has to develop in children in this area of interaction has to do with the way language is used in the classroom. Children need to recognise the emotive and personal nature of language – 'idiot' 'stupid' – and be encouraged to express themselves clearly (though not, therefore, dispassionately). Tone and volume need to be kept under control, not just to avoid a riot, but to ensure that it is discussion which is taking place, and not the subjugation of others.

The skills of taking part in an informative yet lively discussion need to be learned from the start. The art of thinking before speaking, or of organising what one says in some sort of sequence, or of questioning what another person means can ensure that a discussion is a learning experience and not a free-for-all.

This means that teachers need to be aware of what is actually going on in class and group discussion and to make a point of drawing attention to instances where standards of good relationships are being maintained or broken. The teacher's own example is, of course, paramount in this exercise. The teacher's respect for the views of the children in the classroom, a willingness to listen to and share opinions and a readiness to engage in a joint venture of discovery will contribute to building up good relationships between the children themselves.

If these social and interactive skills are not developed, a major part of the task of R.E. in the classroom can be left uncompleted.

Insight and awareness skills

These apparently vague terms are intended to point to some of the sensitivities that children learning R.E. need to cultivate. For what is sought in this subject is not a cold, clinical and distant objectivity, but a real engagement in and appreciation of what one is dealing with. The death of a friend or particular beliefs about human worth and dignity are not simply matters for mechanical analysis, since we are all involved in them at an existential level. Dealing with this level of experience does require insight and awareness, and it is one of the teacher's tasks to cultivate these qualities in children.

One example of this in practice is the need for empathy as a vehicle of understanding. When children are observing other people's behaviour, their understanding of it will be considerably deepened if they are able to grasp something of what it might mean to be participating in it – or at least to have sufficient motivation to want that kind of understanding. As teachers help children to develop this empathy, it will in turn make them more sensitive and responsive to the beliefs and ways of life of people who are different from themselves. It will help them gradually to grow out of initial reactions of rejection or embarrassment in the face of what is strange or unusual.

This ability to share empathetically in someone else's beliefs and actions is sometimes referred to as 'standing in another person's shoes'. There is an obvious sense in which this is impossible, especially for children. It does not mean, however, that we must be imprisoned by the old notion that 'only a Muslim knows what it is like to be a Muslim'. Understanding and empathy can lead us some way along the road, and can certainly deliver us from attitudes based on prejudice and hostility to anything with which we are unfamiliar.

For example, understanding some of the concerns which Muslims and others feel in practising their religion in a strange land and in the midst of a strange people and culture is an important aspect of the kind of awareness children should be developing in R.E. An exercise in which children imagine themselves in a foreign country, with all kinds of language barriers and strange customs, and in which they think of the kind of things that would be important to them, could help to provide a basis for this sort of empathy and understanding. Other imaginative exercises through the use of story, fantasy or role play for example could help to promote this kind of aware-ness of the needs and aspirations of others.

Another area in which insight and awareness are needed is in dealing with the wide variety of ways in which beliefs and ideas are expressed. Most of the ideas of the great traditions are expressed not in any sort of scientific language, but in much more subtle and imprecise ways. They make use of metaphor, simile, myth, legend, allegory, parable, poetry and liturgy, and some of their most important ideas and beliefs are communicated through art, music, drama, movement and symbol. Children need to be encouraged to look for meaning rather than take things at face value, and to be sensitive to the ways in which language and art forms are used and regarded. When handling religious artefacts, for example, they need to be aware of the ways in which they are used by adherents. When visiting a place of worship, they need to be particularly sensitive to the meaning and significance of that place for those who use it.

One of the ways in which insight and awareness can be developed is through the cultivation of the imagination. Not all children have the same ability to use their imagination and it may be that those who have the greatest gift in this direction will be the ones most likely to reach mature understanding. At the same time, it is an essential part of the R.E. teacher's task to provide children with ample opportunity for exploring ideas and experiences in an imaginative way and for using their imaginations to express their responses. This will help to locate the focus of the subject away from a preoccupation with 'learning facts about' and towards the idea of 'learning from' the material being explored.

Skills of evaluation and reflection

Evaluation is essentially a fairly complex process. It begins at a superficial level where a child expresses a personal response to something or someone ('rubbish' or 'great'). It is, however, much more than mere opinion, and if evaluation is to be worthwhile, some thought needs to be given to the skills that can be developed to make it possible. Developing skills of evaluation is essentially an ongoing process, beginning with immediate and unreflective responses, and advancing to a very sophisticated level of critical awareness. The task with children is to sharpen up the processes and criteria by which they evaluate what they are learning.

Evaluation in its root meaning has to do with judging or assessing the value of something, often in relation to other alternatives. Since R.E. is very much concerned with questions of worth and value (they are some of the most important ultimate questions that children consider) it follows that helping children to arrive at more mature evaluations is an important exercise. It is one in which they are in fact never likely to arrive, since the process of sifting and evaluating goes on well after school. Nonetheless, it is certainly of value to them to be aware of how and why they evaluate.

The basic ingredients for helping children to evaluate what they are learning are the knowledge and understanding of the subject, which they are gradually building up, combined with an understanding and awareness of the criteria they are using to make their evaluations. These criteria will, with the help of the teacher, become much more sophisticated as they move from 'It's what I feel' to 'I think this is the most important thing, because . . .' The reasons they give will reflect their own developing beliefs and values, and the skilled teacher will want to be encouraging children all the time to develop their ideas further, so that they do not acquiesce in the thought that there is no further they can go.

The evaluation of which we have been speaking is essentially a cognitive skill and depends largely on a growing ability to be objective. In R.E., however, there is a most important subjective side to the exercise, and that concerns the children's ability to reflect upon what they are exploring. Reflection, in this sense, means asking subjective questions – 'What is there of value in this for me?' 'How does this change the way I look at things?'. Once again, reflection starts at a very early age in terms of immediate feeling responses and can develop to a very mature level.

The teacher of R.E. can once again help children in this process. Reflecting on one's own experience and that of others requires time, patience and – a rare quality – quiet. The teacher can help children to begin to ask the right questions, to avoid superficial responses, to look 'inwards' as well as 'outwards' and to seek opportunities for reflection.

There is a real sense in which the success of R.E. depends on the extent to which a teacher has been able to build up this reflective capacity in children. It is quite clearly a key element in the way children mature in their own beliefs and values and develop a consistent pattern of life.

Commitment

We have already made it clear, in the discussion of the general aim of the subject, that commitment to any one particular set of beliefs cannot be either a prerequisite or a goal of R.E. It is, however, an essential part of the R.E. teacher's aim to encourage a commitment to the value of the search for meaning and identity and to the importance of the task of developing consistent beliefs, attitudes and behaviour. These aims are the rationale of the subject. The teacher of R.E. will, therefore, be concerned to promote enthusiasm for the subject, and to make it interesting and relevant to the needs of the children.

Some of the skills, abilities and attitudes listed here are part of the 'hidden curriculum' of the subject. They are not likely to be specified in any R.E. programme. They will, however, be clearly in the front of the teacher's mind in virtually every lesson, and a conscious effort will be made to reinforce them at every opportunity. On the other hand, particular lessons may be devoted to specific skills, such as understanding symbols, interpreting myths, observing behaviour or recognising propaganda. These will need to be carefully planned into the syllabus.

Final consideration

None of the skills, abilities and attitudes that we have considered here is unique to R.E., but all of them are essential to it. What they do represent is the style, balance and emphasis of the subject. They clearly place the subject at the opposite end of the spectrum from those areas of the curriculum which are primarily concerned with scientific enquiry and analysis, and much closer to those concerned with language and art. At the same time, the contribution of R.E. to the curriculum as a whole is both distinctive and essential.

PART THREE

HOW CAN R.E. BE PLANNED?

So far we have established a principle aim, identified the source of content and examined some of the concepts, skills and attitudes with which the subject is concerned.

The task now is to see how the subject may be planned sequentially in such a way that it offers pupils a balanced programme which has variety, progression and relevance.

1 Two sets of planning principles

It is acknowledged that there can never be one right programme of R.E. to be followed by all pupils in all schools. Many local and individual factors have to be considered when planning particular school programmes. There are, however, several important principles and guidelines which can be applied to the task of sequencing the teaching of the subject. The most important of these arises from an understanding of the way in which children in the classroom develop in their abilities to understand and reflect upon the material they are exploring. The second emerges when the logic of the field of enquiry is related to these understandings of the ways in which children learn.

CHILDREN IN RELATION TO PLANNING

The development of our understanding of the subject has made only slight reference to the question of what might be appropriate for primary, middle or secondary children in R.E. Many of the examples and ideas given so far might be quite unsuitable for five or ten year-olds, and others would be inappropriate for older children.

R.E., like any other subject, depends on an understanding of the fact that teaching must be related to the ability of the children and their appropriate stage of development. In broad terms it is well established that children learn in different ways at different ages, but that it is not possible to relate age to learning development with any precision. It is also recognised that development is not uniform and that there are wide variations in ability between children of the same age. We are therefore well advised to speak only in general terms and to draw broad conclusions about where emphasis should be placed with any given group of children. The emphasis on broad, general categories applies as much to the moral and emotional development of children as it does to their intellectual development. Since R.E. is not simply a cognitive academic exercise, the teacher of R.E. needs to bear all these factors in mind in planning the subject.

We may describe in these general terms three broad stages of learning development through which children in the age range five to sixteen will pass. In the earliest years, most of their learning will be through their own experience of the world around them and through the feelings which this generates. Later, they will begin to extend their horizons through observation and by gathering and organising information. Only when they reach adolescence will they be able to use and explore abstract concepts and general principles. These stages are not discreet but merge into each other, so that it is probably best to think in terms of where the emphasis needs to be placed rather than making sharp distinctions at particular ages. The following diagram is used to illustrate this general distribution of emphasis:

perception. They will become aware that there are certain people, objects, buildings, places, forms of dress, foods, occasions and events that have special importance. They will begin to make simple identifications. The use of story will be important at this stage as a way of arousing their curiosity, encouraging the use of their imagination, and helping them to reflect on their own experience. Stories at this level may be drawn from the religious traditions, so that children may become familiar with them. Gradually children will begin

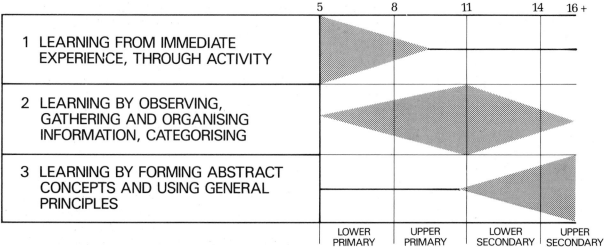

This general scheme for recognising the kind of development of children's understanding which we might expect in R.E. can be expressed in terms of the way children might explore the subject's field of enquiry at the four main stages of schooling:

Infant and lower primary
Infants and lower primary children will begin their R.E. through exploring their own experiences in relation to some of the key topics of shared human experience. They will be encouraged to reflect on their own feelings of pleasure, pain, awe, wonder, mystery, beauty. They will need to find ways of expressing those feelings through movement, music, art. This will provide opportunity for stimulating their imagination. Their curiosity about their own feelings and about people, objects, places and events around them will develop. They will ask questions, some simple, some profound, and they will be encouraged to go on asking questions rather than arriving at solutions.

Some children will have their own experiences of religious groups and activities. They will be encouraged to explore their own experiences and those of others. To begin with, their exploration will be simply at the level of their own sensory

to recognise and explore the differences between themselves and others. The foundations of relationship skills are laid when children are encouraged to accept and value both themselves and these differences, and at the same time to recognise and celebrate a common bond between all people.

The sequence of R.E. teaching at this stage is not of prime importance. Many of the elements may appear to an adult mind to be confusing and disjointed. The R.E., however, can and should be planned in such a way that children are helped to explore as wide a range as possible of those elements of the subject which will later provide a foundation for further exploration. The actual organisation of the subject can be made easier where, for example, the assembly is seen as a way of stimulating children to explore further some of the experiences it deals with; and where topics chosen by the teachers collectively for theme work are of the kind that open up some of those more significant human experiences which are part of the subjects field of enquiry.

Upper primary
At this stage children are no longer dependent on their own sensory perceptions and are able to view

other people in a more objective and detached way. The emphasis will be on gathering information, especially in relation to those topics which are significant for R.E. They will begin to observe relationships between religious activities and to organise and categorise the information they gather. They will begin to use technical terminology and will be able to state beliefs in a simple way. They will need little encouragement to widen their own horizons, observing the way people behave, and exploring their reasons for doing so. They will still find it difficult to appreciate the feelings and experiences of other religious believers; but they may begin to form more coherent ideas of what it means to belong to particular religious traditions, especially through the use of biographical material.

Of special importance at this stage is the development of communication skills which will later help towards a more mature understanding of religion and avoid some of the pitfalls of literalism. Children will explore at a simple level the way language is used to convey religious ideas – how, for example, metaphors are used to describe God, or how stories are told to explain the origins of the world. They will give close attention to the way in which religions use symbols, dramatic rituals, music and art to convey important ideas.

They will also widen the horizons of their understanding of significant human experience, and in particular, begin to see immediate, personal and local questions as aspects of wider, more universal ones. They will identify and make their own responses to some of the problems of being human. They will be encouraged to develop further their ability to ask and pursue more perceptive questions. They will also at this stage become familiar with some of the rules which are used in religion to guide behaviour. This will prepare the ground for a later consideration of how systems of rules and values apply to particular issues in the modern world.

Lower secondary

This stage is not to be sharply distinguished from the upper primary, and the work done in the lower secondary will be a direct progression of work already undertaken. Thus children will continue to develop larger and more comprehensive categories for the material they explore, and will begin to develop the necessary concepts for handling it. In particular, they will explore the beliefs that underlie religious practice and start to draw them together in a coherent pattern. This is an appropriate stage for children to begin to build up a framework of understanding of particular

religions, viewing them as a whole, and being able to relate behaviour, experience and belief to each other. They will begin to understand, for example, how a variety of different rituals all point towards a central core of beliefs and values, and how these in turn shape and inform basic attitudes to life.

They will at this stage continue to develop their understanding of the aesthetic and symbolic elements in religion. It is also an appropriate stage for children to begin their critical appraisal of some of the facts they have been studying. This will apply not only to rules and codes of behaviour, but also to basic beliefs and attitudes. They will need to sharpen up their ability to raise perceptive questions and, in particular, to discuss them constructively with others.

They will now be able to think more deeply about the experience of being human. They will be able to distance this experience further from their own immediate concerns and to think in more abstract terms. Thus they will begin to acquire some understanding of basic concepts which underlie questions (e.g. authority, destiny) and some of the concepts which underlie religious belief (e.g. faith, salvation, non-attachment), so that at a later stage they will be able to perceive the interrelationships which lie at the heart of the subject. These concepts will, however, continue to be acquired through concrete examples.

Upper secondary

At this stage children should be moving towards acquiring a range of more general, abstract concepts, again based on concrete examples. There will be very much less emphasis on collecting basic information and much more on promoting understanding of inner beliefs and attitudes. In particular, children will begin to perceive how religious beliefs and attitudes are closely interrelated with those human experiences which raise ultimate questions. They may now begin to gain understanding of the distinctive features of religious and secular perspectives.

Throughout their R.E. programme they will have recognised the variety of ways in which religious practices and beliefs are expressed. They will now begin to recognise some of the varieties of interpretation and attitude found within religions, e.g. traditional and progressive/radical. This understanding is important, for it is in the upper secondary school that questions of relevance become central to the children's concerns. That is why R.E. at this stage will focus attention particularly on personal and social moral issues which are seen to be of concern and relevance. They also provide one of the best ways for exploring the subject at this level. The issues are explored in R.E. to help children to perceive the ultimate questions they raise and to relate them to some of the varieties of beliefs and teachings of the traditional belief systems. This will also help them in the task of understanding some of the general principles which lie behind rules of behaviour and codes of conduct.

Upper secondary children will be encouraged to evaluate for themselves the beliefs, attitudes and experiences they are exploring. The emphasis will be on developing criteria for critical judgement and sharpening their ability to get to the heart of issues. This should lead not only to an awareness of and respect for the way in which others behave and view life, but also to an understanding of the need for them to develop their own set of beliefs and values and a consistent style of life.

Continuing education
The level and breadth of understanding that might be achieved by the age of sixteen is intended to provide a foundation for continuing education – both the informal learning of the school leaver and the formal learning of the tertiary stage. School leavers should have sufficient knowledge and understanding of religion to recognise and respond to those aspects which might be encountered anywhere at any time, and sufficient awareness to continue to raise questions about, and reflect upon, their own experiences and those of others.

Those who are going on to pursue Religious Studies at a more advanced level will of course have the same basis of knowledge, understanding and awareness for themselves, but they should also have a firm and broad foundation on which to build their future studies. At the tertiary level it is most likely that their areas of study will take them into exploring aspects and perspectives which they have not really touched upon so far. Some of these will involve study in greater depth, others in greater breadth.

At the tertiary stage, therefore, we can expect that traditional belief systems will be explored, for example, in terms of the study of their historical development, or of a detailed study of sacred texts. Both these aspects, which have played a considerable part in R.E. in the primary and secondary phases in the past, are in fact much more appropriate to the tertiary level, since they involve handling language, concepts and varieties of interpretation which are beyond the understanding of younger children. Their studies might also involve them in exploring the psychological, political, sociological and cultural functions of religion. On a broader spectrum, their R.E. in the primary and secondary schools should provide the groundwork for exploring such aspects as the dialogue of faiths and the philosophy of religion.

THE WAY CHILDREN LEARN AND THE LOGIC OF THE FIELD OF ENQUIRY

Throughout the above discussion reference has been made both to what children can learn and to how they might learn it at different stages in their development.

When planning a programme of R.E. and setting it out in terms of a school syllabus, the emphasis should be on what is to be learned. In other words the syllabus should give a clear indication of the subject matter to be explored at each stage of schooling. Taken together across the whole five to sixteen range, this should indicate the way in which children are helped to explore the total field of enquiry in appropriate ways. To achieve this progressive exploration, teachers need to combine this understanding of the logical structure of the field of enquiry with their insights into the ways in which children learn.

Reference to the diagrammatic presentation of the R.E. field of enquiry on page 10 will remind us that there are both observable and hidden aspects of each of the three sources of content and that any understanding of the relationships between these three sources involves grappling with complex and abstract concepts. The outer segments in each circle point to very concrete and observable events and behaviour. The inner circles and the interconnecting arrows suggest far more abstract ideas and experiences. When this is linked to the fact that most people learn by progressing from the concrete to the abstract, a self-evident sequencing pattern emerges. R.E. begins with the observable features of religion and human experience and moves towards those abstract cores of ultimate questions, beliefs and spirituality.

This pattern of sequencing subject matter drawn from the subject's field of enquiry can be refined a little further if we take account of another general principle enunciated above. Children's learning is enhanced when they are helped to relate new knowledge to what is already familiar and within their present experience and comprehension.

The family context is familiar to the majority of children and thus provides a natural reference point to which they can relate new and unfamiliar patterns of behaviour, including those which reflect different religious beliefs. Examples drawn from these segments make very appropriate topics for lower primary children.

Within this lower primary age band (five to eight), children can also begin to use their experience of the school as a small community to relate to information about unfamiliar religious communities.

Reference to very individualistic behaviour patterns can be added during the upper primary years. Topics which reflect the ways in which religious people relate their beliefs to public life can be introduced in the lower secondary years. These can continue into the upper secondary years when direct study of beliefs and spirituality should also be undertaken.

On this basis we can now set out, again in diagrammatic form, a viable sequencing pattern for planning an R.E. syllabus across the five to sixteen age range. Only two of the circles are used because, as previously stressed, the other one points to pupils' and teachers' own individual patterns of belief and behaviour and therefore its inclusion cannot be planned into the curriculum. Material from these sources can only emerge in an ad hoc way within the context of particular lessons.

Lower primary

In the lower primary age band, topics arising from concrete and immediate happenings and experiences in the context of family and community life, including religious community life, would seem to be most appropriate.

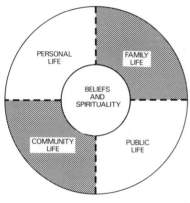

TRADITIONAL BELIEF SYSTEMS

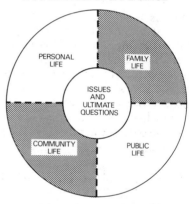

SHARED HUMAN EXPERIENCE

Upper primary

Topics which focus on very personal and individual behaviour and values may be added for children in the upper primary years. By this time their natural self-centredness may have been lessened sufficiently to allow a more objective consideration of such topics.

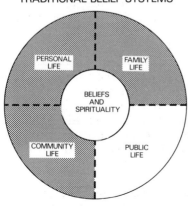

TRADITIONAL BELIEF SYSTEMS

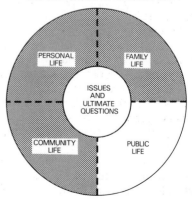

SHARED HUMAN EXPERIENCE

Lower secondary

In the lower secondary years many pupils will be ready to expand this diet to include topics which focus attention on the world community. They may also begin to study some of the ways in which the various belief systems relate central beliefs and values to public life, social structures and international issues.

TRADITIONAL BELIEF SYSTEMS

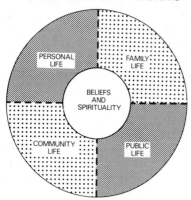

SHARED HUMAN EXPERIENCE

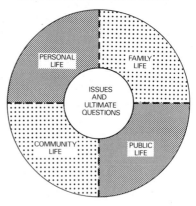

Upper secondary

By the time pupils reach the upper secondary levels, they should be ready to deepen their understanding of the ways in which central beliefs and values relate to public life, social structures and international issues. They should also be ready to explore ultimate questions and particular sets of beliefs and values in a more direct way. They may also be interested in examining in some detail and depth, the relationships between the three areas of content. The double-headed arrows in the three-circle diagram indicate the substance of this complex relationship.

TRADITIONAL BELIEF SYSTEMS

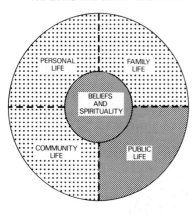

SHARED HUMAN EXPERIENCE

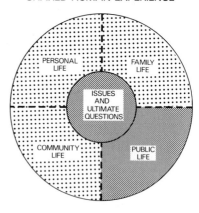

These diagrams are not, of course, meant to represent an inflexible pattern of progression. They are intended primarily to suggest where emphasis should be placed in planning. Primary children will certainly be raising ultimate questions and thinking about beliefs, and upper secondary children may well be exploring aspects of the family context. The diagrams indicate where the emphasis is most appropriately placed.

2 Two approaches to planning

Over recent years two quite distinct, yet interrelated approaches to the teaching of R.E. in schools have been developed. Both of these approaches are valid and useful ways of exploring the subject's field of enquiry and for achieving its general aims and specific objectives.

A well-balanced programme of R.E. will give children opportunities to learn from both approaches. However, it is essential that in planning and presenting learning experiences, teachers are quite clear about the nature and purpose of each approach and about which one is being followed in any teaching situation. A failure to distinguish between the two almost inevitably results in confused teaching and muddled understanding on the part of pupils. The different objectives of the two approaches are important, since they will clearly determine the way in which relevant content is selected and used.

THE SYSTEMS APPROACH

In this approach to the subject, the focus of attention is on just one of the systems. Children are being helped to develop an understanding of, for example, Christianity. Of course, there is no suggestion that the totality of the system is being explored under one particular topic – not even the whole school programme could provide sufficient time for that. The topic should deal with one particular aspect of the system, and not simply provide a springboard for leaping off onto other aspects. The Systems approach does, however, enable the teachers to plan for a gradual building up by the children of a reasonably comprehensive picture of a particular system.

Although the main focus under this approach is on one particular system, the nature of the subject demands that links should be made with shared

THE SYSTEMS APPROACH   THE R.E. FIELD OF ENQUIRY

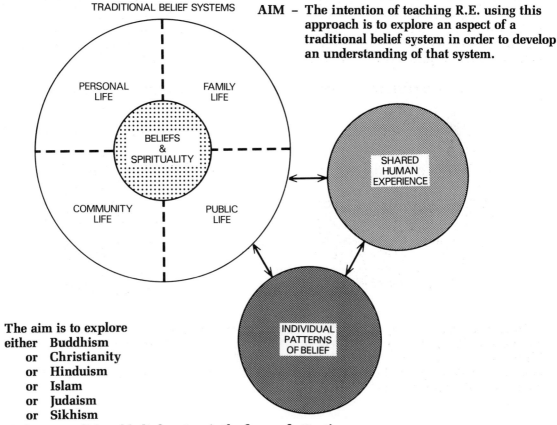

TRADITIONAL BELIEF SYSTEMS

PERSONAL LIFE · FAMILY LIFE · BELIEFS & SPIRITUALITY · COMMUNITY LIFE · PUBLIC LIFE

SHARED HUMAN EXPERIENCE

INDIVIDUAL PATTERNS OF BELIEF

AIM – **The intention of teaching R.E. using this approach is to explore an aspect of a traditional belief system in order to develop an understanding of that system.**

The aim is to explore
either **Buddhism**
    or **Christianity**
    or **Hinduism**
    or **Islam**
    or **Judaism**
    or **Sikhism**
Only *one* traditional belief system is the focus of attention.

human experience and with the ideas and experiences of the children in the classroom. This should not be done in a merely artificial way. The aspect of human experience should arise clearly and centrally from the aspect of the traditional belief system under consideration. This aspect of human experience should in turn provide a link with the children's own concerns and experiences.

Let us take, for example, lessons dealing with Christian baptism using the Systems approach. Various aspects of this topic can be dealt with in both the primary and the secondary school. Since we are following the Systems approach the main and essential focus of the work will be on building up an understanding of the various practices and beliefs associated with baptism. This in turn, along with a range of other topics on other aspects of Christianity, will help children gradually to build up their understanding of Christianity as a whole.

Work on the topic of baptism may explore some of the rituals, symbols and stories associated with this practice, the roles, intentions and experiences of the participants and the Christian beliefs and values which underlie it. At the same time, there are a number of important themes which arise from a consideration of baptism and which help to relate this specifically Christian practice with wider human experiences and questions. For example, the themes of welcome, belonging, responsibility, commitment, identity and hope all represent important dimensions of the practice of baptism and point to the links with human experiences. Some of the links may be more appropriately explored at primary level, others at secondary level. At the lower primary level, for example, the theme of welcome may be dominant.

At the same time, children in the classroom will not simply be exploring the topic and its related themes as a detached, objective piece of study. For some, the actual practices of baptism will be part of their own experience and awareness. They may have seen or participated in a baptism service, and may have their own unique perceptions of it. For others, baptism will appear strange and unfamiliar. For all of them, however, the themes and the questions they raise will provide material for reflecting on their own experiences, and the ideals, beliefs and values associated with Christian baptism will provide one of the sources through which they will refine their own beliefs and values.

It is not necessary for these links to be carefully and elaborately worked out and dwelt upon at every level. The stages by which the links are made are progressive and it is only at the upper secondary stage, at the earliest, where the nature of the links is explored in its own right. Thus, while the links remain throughout the R.E. curriculum, the essential focus of the Systems approach is on the understanding of one particular system.

THE LIFE THEMES APPROACH

A topic dealt with under this approach will focus quite clearly on helping children to explore and understand an aspect of human experience. In this case the teacher may draw upon quite a range of examples in order to illustrate and illuminate the topic. As a topic appropriate to R.E. it will have potential for raising ultimate questions and for that reason there will be important links with the traditional belief systems. For it is these systems whose beliefs, values and practices serve to interpret, support and challenge human experience and the questions it raises.

In most cases, therefore, the illustrations which are chosen to illuminate the topic will be drawn from the traditional belief systems. These will need to be set alongside other illustrations drawn from more general human experience in order to highlight the meaning and importance of the topic. The emphasis here is on variety. It therefore follows that illustrations drawn from traditional belief systems will reflect this variety. In other words the topic should be illustrated from the beliefs and practices of more than one of the systems.

Let us take as an example work which might be done on the theme of 'caring'. The theme has good potential for R.E. since it opens up important questions about meaning and value. The theme is suitable at both primary and secondary levels. Children might begin to develop their understanding of the theme by considering ways in which others care for them, and how the care is shown, gradually widening their understanding by exploring other examples – caring for the sick, lonely or poor, the way communities care for one another, organised and informal caring. There are clear links with traditional belief systems and examples of different forms of caring will be drawn from various traditions – the langar as an expression of the caring work of the Sikh community, or the way in which Muslims care for the poor in their communities through the distribution of Zakat, or the example of Christian caring found in the work of Mother Teresa of Calcutta.

At the secondary level, the same theme may be explored by using other concrete examples to raise some of the issues related to the theme of 'care'. Why should we care? What is the best way to show care? Is justice better than charity? Who is my

AIM – The intention of teaching R.E. using this approach is to explore an aspect of shared human experience in order to develop an understanding of that experience and the ultimate questions it raises.

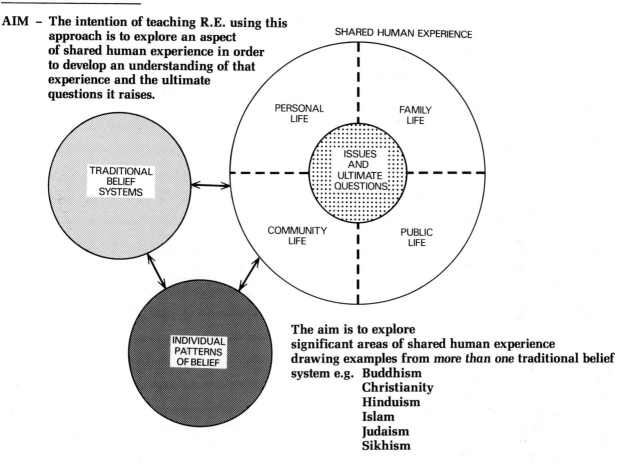

SHARED HUMAN EXPERIENCE

PERSONAL LIFE

FAMILY LIFE

ISSUES AND ULTIMATE QUESTIONS

TRADITIONAL BELIEF SYSTEMS

COMMUNITY LIFE

PUBLIC LIFE

INDIVIDUAL PATTERNS OF BELIEF

The aim is to explore significant areas of shared human experience drawing examples from *more than one* traditional belief system e.g. **Buddhism**
Christianity
Hinduism
Islam
Judaism
Sikhism

neighbour? Illustrations from traditional belief systems should demonstrate the different ways in which they serve to interpret, support and challenge the human experience of the need for caring – values such as love and compassion, and ideas such as the belief that God cares.

As with the Systems approach the concern is not merely to examine and study what is 'out there' but to help children to look at some of the questions and implications of the human experience of caring for themselves and for their own values, beliefs and style of life. Thus in this approach also there are important links between the three areas of the field of enquiry. The emphasis, however, in the Life Themes approach is on developing our understanding of the theme and of the questions and issues it raises, not on learning about particular traditional belief systems. In this case the concrete examples (Mother Teresa, zakat and the langar) are introduced in order to broaden the concept of caring; not to study the wider beliefs and practices of Sikhism, Islam and Christianity.

DIFFERENTIATING BETWEEN THE TWO APPROACHES WHEN PROGRAMME PLANNING

The difference between the two approaches should be apparent from the examples already given above. It does mean that a common topic could be included in both a Systems approach and a Life Themes approach, but the purpose of its inclusion and the way it is used in the classroom will differ.

The topic of baptism is a case in point. In a Systems approach what is important is the way in which an exploration of the topic helps towards an understanding of Christianity. In a Life Themes approach, however, baptism might appear in a number of contexts by way of illustration, depending on the theme chosen. For example, a theme of 'welcoming' could include reference to baptism as an example. What is being explored here is the way in which welcome to a new child is expressed in the baptism of infants. What is *not* being explored is all the detail of the service, the symbols used, the people who participate, or the Christian beliefs that underlie the service, *unless* they are material to the theme of welcome.

In contrast, another theme such as responsibility could include a reference to baptism as an illustration. In this case, the emphasis of the exploration would be firmly on the promises made by the parents and the way in which the service serves to heighten their awareness of their responsibility for loving and nurturing a newborn child. Other aspects of the service may be material to the theme – the responsibility of the community to support the family, for example – but the purpose of the exercise is to focus attention on the way Christians interpret *responsibility*, not on the details of the baptism service.

At the same time, the Christian interpretation of responsibility expressed in the baptism service will be just one example amongst others. We might include an example from Buddhism – the responsibility of the laity to maintain the sangha, and one from Judaism – the responsibility of children to care for their parents in old age, expressed through the particular example of an extended Jewish family. In all cases, the purpose of the exercise is not to explore the details of Christian, Buddhist or Jewish practice, but to illuminate the theme of responsibility, the ultimate questions it raises, and some of the responses that are given to these questions.

Careful regard to the distinctions between the two approaches will avoid some of the confusions that could arise. These are most common where a theme (such as 'welcome') touches on the example (such as 'baptism') but then goes on to explore other aspects of that example in detail, rather than concentrating on the theme.

The danger of this kind of confusion is very obvious in the attempts of some teachers to deal with religions thematically; that is, to organise teaching on the basis of themes which appear to be common to all or most religious traditions (pilgrimage, worship, festivals etc.). We suspect that this approach usually distorts the traditions and does little to develop children's understanding of the subject. It is far better to be quite clear which approach is being used, and therefore to be clear what the objective of exploring the topic is really supposed to be. Thus it is better to be specific and deal with pilgrimage in Islam, or Christians celebrating Holy Communion, or a Jewish family at Passover time as topics under the Systems approach, in order to build up an understanding of Islam or Christianity or Judaism. On the other hand, a topic such as celebration could be used under the Life Themes approach. The purpose of

this topic would be to explore and raise questions about the human capacity to celebrate, the way in which people and events are highly valued, and how people express their joy and identity together. Passover, Easter, Ramadan, Diwali could then furnish examples of celebration, but only to illuminate the theme and the questions, not to provide a lead into explaining particular religions.

EXAMPLES OF THE TWO APPROACHES

It may be useful to draw together the basic principles of the stages of children's development and the two approaches to R.E., and to clarify them by taking example topics.

The example in Table 5 relates to the topic of Passover which is explored according to the Systems approach. The example in Table 6 (page 44) is a consideration of belonging following the Life Themes approach.

The emphasis in each example is focussed on what may be explored, i.e. the kind of content that might be suitable at the different stages of development. In each case possible links with the other areas of the field of enquiry are given as suggestions.

Making sense of the examples
The examples given here suggest not only the kind of content which could be used at each of the age levels, but also some of the processes which might be appropriate to encourage learning. The relevant processes are suggested in each case by the words in italics. The links with the other areas of the field of enquiry arise directly out of the content and processes, and are not merely incidental to them. At the same time it is important to remember that the links are illustrative. They are certainly not the only possible examples of links. But the main focus in both approaches is on the basic content. Thus it can be seen clearly that the purpose of the work done under the Systems approach is to learn more about and build up an understanding of Judaism and the purpose of the teaching and learning under the Life Themes approach is to explore what it means to belong, and to build up an understanding of the concept of identity.

With this distinction in mind, the basic guidelines about how the example links are used become clearer. For instance, the links with traditional belief systems under the theme of belonging show that variety in the examples is important. It is not the prime task here to build up detailed understanding of the various traditions, but rather to provide varied examples of what it

	POSSIBLE CONTENT . . .	. . . LINKED WITH . . .	
		shared human experience	individual patterns of belief
TABLE 5 An example of the Systems approach – Topic: Passover			
LOWER PRIMARY	*Sharing* in a simple Seder meal – *becoming familiar* with the dry *taste* of matzah, the bitter taste of herbs, the sweet taste of charoset – *hearing the story* of Passover night – *singing* some of the *songs* used on this occasion – *listening* to the young children's *questions* – *playing* at finding the afikomen	Enjoying important occasions together	What I have to share and enjoy
UPPER PRIMARY	*Finding out* about chametz – *learning the details* of the Seder meal, and the order of the various parts – *acting the roles* of the various members of the family – *exploring the meanings* given to each of the special foods and the cups of wine – *finding out* about other aspects of the Passover celebrations – *reading* the story of the Exodus	Following customs Conveying meaning through symbols	Customs that are important to me
LOWER SECONDARY	*Exploring* important Jewish *beliefs* (expressed in the Passover celebrations) – e.g. The Chosen People (the Haggadah); the Torah (Mitzvoth relating to Passover); the Messiah (Elijah's cup) – *recognising* important Jewish *values* (the family); *understanding concepts* e.g. tradition (reliving the past)	Keeping rules Sharing beliefs about ourselves and the world we live in	Rules and beliefs I live by
UPPER SECONDARY	*Understanding the importance* for Jews of their sense of identity (noting some cultural variations in the celebration of Passover); *exploring the reasons* why freedom is so important to Jews (related to the prayers for persecuted Jews); *appreciating* Jewish *hopes* and *aspirations* for the future ('next year in Jerusalem')	Celebrating freedom Hoping in the future	What makes me free? What do I hope for?

		...LINKED WITH...	
TABLE 6 **An example of the Life Themes approach – Topic: Belonging**			
	POSSIBLE CONTENT...	traditional belief systems	individual patterns of belief
LOWER PRIMARY	*Sharing* some of the important things that belong to us – *talking* about some of the special people/groups that we belong to – *singing songs* expressing the happiness of belonging – *thinking about* ways in which other people love, care for and protect us – *listening* to stories on these themes	*Stories* illustrating the themes e.g. Guru Nanak and his friends; the prodigal son; Gautama's journey from his palace; Uncle Abu Talib. *Songs* – e.g. 'Shalom Havarim'	What helps me feel secure? Who do I belong to? How can I show that I belong?
UPPER PRIMARY	*Finding out about* the great diversity of families, groups and societies to which people belong – *exploring categories* of belonging in terms of importance – *learning* some of the distinctive *features* of particular groups (dress, behaviour, customs) – *considering the meaning* of 'being British'	*Finding out* what it means to belong to, e.g. a Jewish family (special rules about food), or local Sikh community (dress), or the Christian Church (obligations)	Who do I belong to *most*? Why am I different?
LOWER SECONDARY	*Exploring what it means* to belong in terms of rules, norms, values, constraints, possibilities; *understanding what it means* to belong to socially unacceptable groups – and what it feels like to have no sense of belonging	*Exploring* different kinds of group rules, e.g. rules associated with caste; the Five Pillars of Islam; the Precepts of the Buddha; (also e.g. the 227 rules of the Vinaya).	Whose 'group rules' do I follow? How important are these rules to me?
UPPER SECONDARY	*Considering examples* of conflicts of loyalty within groups – *appreciating* how belonging to a group shapes one's sense of *identity* and *awareness* of those who belong to other groups – *understanding* the ways in which *beliefs influence* groups.	*Considering ideas* of inclusion and exclusivism, e.g. in Islam and Christianity: *tensions* experienced by e.g. Sikhs in British culture.	What are my values? What conflicts of loyalty am I aware of? How can I resolve them? What do I believe about people who belong to other groups/societies?

means to belong. Thus, at the upper primary level, finding out what it means to belong to a Jewish family, a local Sikh community and the Christian Church provides a variety of examples of belonging. Distinctive features of a Jewish family might be explored through the concrete example of dietary rules. Distinctive features of a local Sikh community might be explored through the concrete example of dress, and so on. The purpose of these illustrations is not to focus attention on the details of them, nor on their wider ramifications for the communities in question, but to illustrate different features at different levels and within different contexts to which people belong.

Similarly, at the lower secondary level, the illustrations given are designed to provide varied examples of different kinds of group rules. Some have to do, for example, with 'who you can mix with' or 'who you can marry' (caste rules). Others are very general, and concern basic principles for one's whole life (the Five Pillars of Islam or the Precepts of the Buddha – which provide an interesting contrast). Others are very detailed (the 227 rules followed by Buddhist monks). There is no question here of looking at the rules in great detail, or of understanding the place of the sangha in Buddhism, but simply of recognising that some people's sense of belonging is governed by very detailed and precise rules covering every aspect of a person's life.

The purpose of the links, therefore, is gradually to build up an understanding of the interrelationship between fundamental human experiences, concerns and questions on the one hand, and the basic ideas, beliefs, values and practices of traditional belief systems on the other hand. The emphasis, it will be noted, is on *building up* an understanding. In the earlier stages of schooling the links are there, but only implicitly as far as the children are concerned. They will usually not become explicit until children are much older. It is essential, however, that the teacher has a very clear grasp of the way in which the links operate. Such a conception on the part of the teacher is of paramount importance in understanding the structure of the subject, and therefore in planning how to teach it.

It has already been made clear that the examples of the two approaches given above are highly artificial. It is most unlikely that any teacher would consider dealing with these particular topics in such a methodically sequential fashion, nor is it desirable that they should do so. The examples do, however, help to illustrate the principle that anything may be taught at any age, provided that

the structure of teaching and learning has been clearly grasped by the teacher. They also show the way in which the 'spiral curriculum' nature of R.E. can operate in practice. Broad general concepts and ideas are built up from limited concrete examples, and it is possible to use the same basic topic in a number of different ways at different levels of understanding.

On the other hand, as we indicate below, a balanced programme of R.E. would involve a mixture of the two approaches, and would make use of a variety of contexts for exploring topics as the best way of achieving the subject's overall aim.

BALANCING THE APPROACHES WHEN PROGRAMME PLANNING

The two approaches we have considered represent different ways of exploring the R.E. field of enquiry. The emphasis so far has been very much on the differences between them. The whole point of the differences is to make clear that there are different intentions and objectives in each case, and that a clear understanding of the distinctions will help greatly when it comes to planning topics in R.E.

At the same time, the two approaches both remain faithful to the essential nature of the subject, for they enable relevant links to be made between the three areas of the field of enquiry. However, in an overall programme of R.E., it is also essential that a balance is achieved between the two approaches. This balance is important for two reasons.

Firstly, although it is perfectly possible to plan a complete R.E. programme using just one approach, such a scheme is likely to distort the essential nature of the subject – and it is likely to lack the variety which is also an important ingredient in R.E. A programme of R.E. restricted entirely to the Systems approach may leave children with the impression that belief systems are really conglomerates of strange practices and unusual ideas followed by particular groups of people who happen to think them important. They may fail to see and experience something of the force and urgency of those aspects of human experience to which they relate.

On the other hand, a programme based entirely on the Life Themes approach has the obvious limitation that children are unlikely to develop a systematic conception of any traditional belief system. They may have a wide knowledge and sensitive appreciation of life's puzzles and mysteries. They will not have a clear and coherent understanding of some of the great belief systems which have inspired and challenged countless people for generations.

The second reason why balance is important has to do with the way in which children's understanding develops. In the youngest years of schooling, children learn primarily from their own immediate experiences and those of people around them. This suggests that some of the kind of themes which can be dealt with through the Life Themes approach will be most suitable for them. There is no need, to begin with, for a carefully structured and systematic programme. This in fact accords well with the kind of approach to teaching in general which we find in most infant and lower primary classes.

The middle years of schooling are, for reasons already suggested, particularly suited to the gathering and organisation of information. This suggests that the Systems approach can be especially helpful in these years as a means of building up children's knowledge and understanding of particular systems.

Towards the end of secondary schooling, when questions of meaning, application and relevance assume primary importance, it is likely that the Life Themes approach will be found most useful. It will also, of course, be the period of schooling where a more integrated understanding of the R.E. field of enquiry will be expected.

This overall pattern is a question of emphasis rather than strict linear development. It does nevertheless serve as a guideline when planning the school R.E. programme. The balance of emphasis in the use of the two approaches may be represented in the following diagram.

Balance of emphasis in the use of the two approaches 5 – 16

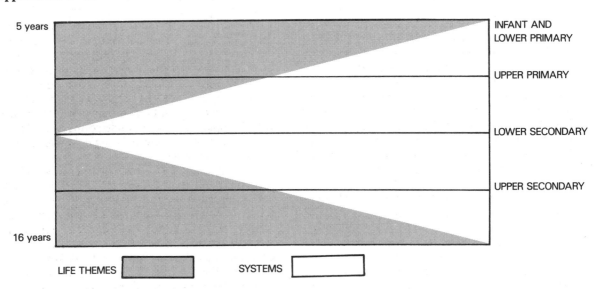

3 Identifying suitable topics for R.E. when programme planning

When teachers are planning their programme of R.E., it is clear that they need to be able to break down the subject into manageable topics. This is necessarily an artificial exercise, but it can make a useful contribution to children's understanding. The basic principles for selecting material for R.E., and for relating it to children's levels of understanding and ability, have already been considered.

It is important to recognise that there is no definitive list of topics that will fit the situation of every school. At the same time, the kind of topics which could usefully be covered in the classroom are suggested in the supplementary manuals. The purpose of this section is simply to reiterate some important points to consider in identifying topics.

CHOOSING THE RIGHT SORT OF TOPICS

Any topic that is chosen must have potential for exploring an aspect of the subject's field of enquiry. It must be clear from the title of the topic which area of the field of enquiry is being explored, and which approach is being used.

For these reasons it is best to avoid stating topics purely in terms of the subject matter being considered. A title such as 'Holy Communion' is misleading. It gives no indication of what, precisely, children are to explore about Holy Communion. The same would apply to the title 'Poverty'.

For example, the title 'Sharing a special Christian meal' indicates more clearly that the experience of sharing is the focus of the topic, and that the purpose is not to explore in great detail what happens on this occasion. It is therefore an appropriate lower primary topic. On the other hand, the title 'Celebrating the Mass in a Roman Catholic church' suggests that we are looking at what happens in church, and looking at the details of the service. This would be a suitable upper primary topic. Alternatively, we could take the title 'What is a sacrament?' In this case we would be considering the concept of sacrament and using Holy Communion as an illustration. In each case Holy Communion is the subject matter but the different titles clearly indicate the level at which it is being explored and what aspect is being considered.

Similarly, titles such as 'What does it feel like to be poor?' 'Why are there poor people in the world?' and 'Attitudes to poverty' are far more indicative than simply using the word 'Poverty'.

As a further example of the importance of stating topics in a more precise form, we might refer back to the last section where we were considering the two approaches to R.E. using the general topics of 'Passover' and 'Belonging.' Neither of these, as titles, gives any real indication of what the exploration is intended to achieve. If, however, they are set out in the kind of form given below, the intention becomes much clearer. This clarity makes the planning of the subject much more precise and indicates what the subject is all about. Another reason for making topics as specific as possible is that it avoids the danger of allowing a topic to become a peg on which any apparently connected (and often unconnected) idea can be hung.

TOPICS IN THE PRIMARY SCHOOL

The last point is particularly pertinent to the situation of R.E. in the primary school. There is, of course, a very wide range of practice as far as the primary curriculum as a whole is concerned, and as far as R.E. itself is concerned. There are also certain attitudes among some primary teachers which militate against a well-planned and clearly structured R.E. programme.

In most primary schools, the day is divided between work on specific areas and theme work. The ratio of the two varies considerably. R.E. can and should form part of the specific 'subject' work that can be done in the primary school. This does not mean telling an unconnected story, unrelated to anything else that has happened, at the end of the day. There is plenty of material and there are suitable topics through which primary children from the age of five onwards begin to explore the R.E. field of enquiry.

R.E. may, of course, also be incorporated in theme work. Here, however, caution is necessary. A common pattern in primary schools is for a theme to be selected and then explored in a number of dimensions, such as mathematics, language, environmental studies, science, art and crafts, R.E., personal development, etc. The key to this exercise is the choice of theme. If it is of any value, it should be a theme worth exploring in itself, for which the various dimensions provide illumination, and opportunities for exploration as well as

SYSTEMS: PASSOVER		LIFE THEMES: BELONGING
Lower primary	Enjoying Passover	We all belong to someone
Upper primary	Learning about the Seder meal	Learning about groups to which people belong
Lower secondary	Exploring the meaning of Passover	What does it mean to belong?
Upper secondary	The importance of Passover for Jewish people	Identity and belonging

skill development. If, however, the theme is not carefully chosen, teachers may be forced to bend the topic to fit the theme, or stretch the dimension of the theme to fit the topic, in ways which destroy the educational potential of both. R.E. is especially prone to this treatment.

The fact is that some themes are suitable for treatment in R.E. while others are not. Some have a high potential for fulfilling the aims and objectives of R.E., others have a very low potential. Some examples may help to clarify this difficulty.

Themes such as 'myself', 'people who care' and 'harvest' have a relatively high potential for R.E. They are themes which enable children to explore aspects of the subject's field of enquiry and which have potential, sooner or later, for opening up ultimate questions and matters of belief and value. Themes such as 'plants' or 'our neighbourhood' may have potential for R.E., but it very much depends how they are handled. If the theme of 'plants' opens up questions about the wonder of the natural order, and if 'our neighbourhood' helps children to explore, for example, particularly important groups or buildings in the locality ('the local church', 'the mosque' etc.), then they have good potential for R.E. On the other hand, themes such as 'farming' or 'transport' have very low potential for R.E. unless they are handled in a very subtle way by a very perceptive teacher – and the chances are that the subtlety will be quite lost on children.

The great danger is that teachers may take some of these very low-potential themes and try to force some R.E. into them. That is why we still (occasionally, we hope) come across a consideration of Jesus as the Good Shepherd or the parable of the sower tucked into some rural theme and, worse still, transport in ancient Palestine or bullock-carts of the Bible as the R.E. element in 'transport'. The last two examples on transport are so completely irrelevant to the aims and objectives of R.E. as to be meaningless – and they have very little potential as history. The other two examples of the Good Shepherd and the sower as R.E. topics under 'farming' are slightly more subtle, but equally meaningless as R.E. The point is that, in terms of their meaning, the notion of Jesus as the Good Shepherd and the parable of the sower have nothing whatsoever to do with 'farming'. The metaphor of 'Shepherd' has to do with 'leadership' and 'service' or 'care' and the idea of Jesus as the Good Shepherd could, possibly, be introduced if children were looking at those themes. The point of the parable of the sower is, in fact, fairly sophisticated, and depends on an understanding of the differences between parables and allegories.

There is, of course, no reason why young children should not hear the story of the sower. In this case they will simply be enjoying it as a story for the pleasure it gives and the impression it leaves. It is, however, much more appropriate to consider it under a heading such as 'stories Jesus told'; it may then be enjoyed in the same way as other stories told by other important religious leaders.

It is essential, therefore, that primary teachers are absolutely clear what they are trying to achieve in R.E., so that they can see the relevance or otherwise of particular themes. It may be the case – indeed, we suspect it is frequently – that there are very few topics which lend themselves to exploration in all the dimensions of a traditional flow chart. A much more varied approach to theme work is needed. This may result in some subjects being dealt with in one way, others in another. Some may have no worthwhile R.E. dimension to them, and there is no point trying to force it in. Much better, we would argue, to look at a quite separate R.E. topic that really helps to develop understanding than to try to force it into a mould in which it will not fit.

The same general point also applies to the primary practice of devising 'topic webs'. R.E. suffers in the same way when attempts are made to incorporate what is ostensibly R.E. material purely by word association with the theme in question. It is quite possible, simply by the process of word association, to move right away from the main topic, so that some of the material being considered bears absolutely no meaningful relationship to the theme.

It is probably partly on account of this complexity, and the difficulty in identifying suitable themes, that in some cases responsibility for R.E. in the primary curriculum is largely abrogated, and its place recognised merely by an unrelated and unconnected story at the end of the day or by the excuses that 'we do it in assembly' or 'R.E. is going on all the time'. None of these is satisfactory. R.E. may legitimately be taught in its own right from the infant stage onwards, and it may be meaningfully incorporated in carefully chosen themes. While it is perfectly true that it is pointless to try to draw subject boundaries around a lot of work done in the primary school, it is essential that the contribution of the subject areas is both recognised and planned.

THE LOCAL SITUATION

Much of what has been discussed so far, with regard to planning the subject and choosing topics, has been in the context of the ideal situation. That is not usually the reality with which teachers have to work. There are many local considerations and constraints which can make the subject either much easier, or much more difficult, to teach. Such is the nature of curriculum development. No development can take place unless it does so within the opportunities and constraints of the real situation. Neither can it take place unless there is some attempt to change the local situation in such a way that the teaching comes nearer to the real intentions of the subject. A dialogue is essential. This section simply recognises some of those local considerations which have to be taken into account in planning R.E. in schools.

The following are of particular relevance here:

The local education authority agreed syllabus of Religious Education

At the time of writing this still remains the legal basis of R.E. in any given authority. Depending on how it has been drawn up (and when!), it may be a liberating or restricting influence. It is still important, for a variety of reasons, that the teaching of R.E. in a local authority should be seen to be related to its syllabus. That is one reason why the R.E. set out in this manual is intended to support the kind of R.E. promoted in a wide range of up-to-date agreed syllabuses.

The school's policy

There are a thousand and one ways of organising the school curriculum, and this is reflected in the usual tensions between central control and teacher autonomy, or subject orientation and integration or 'education for its own sake' and 'education for the needs of society'. This will inevitably mean that the place of R.E. in the curriculum of each school will vary. That it should have its proper status alongside other subject areas should not be open to question. But in some cases this will mean quite different styles of time-tabling, and if R.E. is seen as part of an integrated whole it will mean that careful thought will have to be given to the basis and purpose of integration.

The school's social context and environment

One of the factors which will determine how R.E. is taught, as well as, to some extent, what is taught, will be the school's social context. In many ways R.E. is much easier to teach in a culturally diverse urban environment than in a culturally monochrome rural setting. The local context may well determine where the emphasis has to be placed simply on account of the availability of suitable local resources in the community. And it would follow that where ninety per cent of the school population is Sikh, then a study of Sikhism in the educational context of the school should feature prominently (but certainly not exclusively) in the R.E. programme.

The available resources

The realities of the school's capitation and the way 'the cake is divided' will be crucial matters in determining what can be included in the R.E. programme. This does not mean that there are indispensable resources, nor that the ingenious teacher cannot find ways of making something come alive for children without having access to the most sophisticated technology and techniques. It does recognise that the availability of resources is important and also that, in reality, good resources are often the point of departure for worthwhile curriculum development.

Teacher expertise

Since the teacher is the most important resource available to the children, it is essential that the teacher of R.E. in the secondary school, and the subject co-ordinator in the primary school, have a clear understanding of what they are doing and why they are doing it. But no teacher can be an inexhaustible compendium of knowledge, and it is recognised that many of those who do teach the subject have not been trained for that purpose. While this is to be regretted, one has to recognise this constraint on the R.E. curriculum and work to the strengths of teachers, rather than their weaknesses. This must not, however, become an excuse for not allowing both the time and the opportunity for teachers to develop new areas of expertise.

PART FOUR

HOW CAN R.E. BE TAUGHT?

Our concentration so far has been on identifying and organising appropriate content in R.E. This is entirely proper in a manual which claims to guide teachers towards a full understanding of the distinctive nature and purpose of R.E. as a subject in schools.

However, the quality of teaching, or the methods of directing pupil learning, adopted by teachers are crucial if the subject matter is to come alive and be processed by pupils in a way which genuinely contributes to their instruction.

Of course, very few teaching styles and methods are specific to any one subject. Wise teachers learn from each other, as well as from books, in order to expand their repertoire of creative and successful techniques for planning and presenting lessons and creating opportunities for learning.

In this section we offer some broad guidelines which will help the progression from the planning of the overall school programme in R.E. to the task of designing and presenting R.E. lessons which are consistent with the nature and aims of the subject and appropriate to the needs and interests of different groups of pupils in schools.

1 Designing units of work

WHAT IS MEANT BY A UNIT OF WORK?

There are several levels at which a subject in school may be planned and organised. As far as R.E. is concerned, this process actually starts outside school with the local authority's agreed syllabus. This, however, may provide relatively little guidance about how general principles and broad areas can be translated into the school and the classroom. Here the first stage of planning, logically, is the school's R.E. syllabus which presents an overview of the teaching of the subject right across the age range. The syllabus is then broken down into years and terms, where the general themes for these divisions can be set out. Within each year and term, a number of more specific topics will be covered, and these in turn will be broken down into lessons.

Ideally, the school syllabus will state, within each year, the topics to be covered. These will be set out in the kind of form suggested in the last Part. The work on that topic may range over a number of lessons, in some cases only one or two, in others five or six. The number is not important. This series of lessons is referred to here as a unit of work. It is a short series of learning experiences which has a self-contained purpose and its own specific, short-term objectives, and which at the same time makes a contribution to the overall educational aim of the subject.

Thus, for example, a unit of work may be entitled 'Learning about the Seder meal.' The number of lessons needed to cover this topic will depend on the teacher's assessment of its importance within the overall syllabus, as well as on a range of other considerations. It is possible however that the unit of work could be broken down into two or three lessons covering different aspects, or exploring the topic in different ways.

Unit of work

There is no one right way of setting out the details of a particular unit of work for pupils in schools.

The one offered below contains the essential characteristics suggested in the definition and provides an effective means for communicating to other teachers what the unit is all about and how it might be taught in different situations.

The discipline of designing all units of work within the school programme, in a format such as the one offered here, not only provides a useful guide to all teachers involved in the programme but ensures that the R.E. curriculum is clearly structured, developmental without being repetitive, and accessible for close scrutiny and regular evaluation and improvement.

Approach

In the previous chapter we outlined two different, though related, approaches to the task of planning units of work in R.E.: the Systems and Life Themes approaches. Each approach has its own distinctive emphasis, mixture of content drawn from the total field of enquiry, and its own purpose in relation to the general aim of the subject.

When designing particular units of work it is essential that teachers are clear in their own minds about which approach is being followed. A failure to do this often results in confused thinking and presentation and a serious imbalance in the programme as experienced by the pupils. The approach we adopt will therefore determine what we are trying to achieve through a particular topic.

Topic

The topic should be a brief heading designating the piece of content that is being used as the focus for exploration. The wording of this heading is particularly important since it defines a specific area for exploration. The basic criteria for the choice of topic should be that it is worthwhile in itself as an area of exploration, and that it has the best potential for achieving the objectives and furthering children's understanding. In the case of units of work following the Systems approach, the choice of topics will be determined by these criteria, and by the nature of the tradition being studied. In other words, topics will be related to the kind of themes and areas that are important within that tradition. For example, beliefs about God and theistic spirituality will be explored while studying most religious traditions. However, these would be inappropriate topics when studying the Buddhist tradition, as they are not central to that system.

Content overview

The purpose of writing an overview is to give a succinct summary, in teacher language, of what the unit is all about in terms of its general aim, content or subject matter. Teachers can use this exercise to clarify in their own minds, and to convey clearly to other teachers, the basic intentions of the unit. The kind of elements which might be included in this summary are:

- Where does this topic fit into the field of enquiry?
- Why is it being explored with children in this age range?
- How does this unit relate to previous and future units in advancing children's understanding?

Objectives

The writing of educational or teaching objectives is notoriously difficult. Such statements have to be couched in clear, unambiguous language and capable of translation into practical classroom activities. It should also be possible to assess the extent to which they have been achieved. Of course, R.E. shares the responsibility of making a contribution, parallel to those of other subjects, to the achievement of many general educational objectives. The promotion of good habits in personal organisation, attentive listening, careful observation, respect for truth, appreciation of intellectual, creative and imaginative pursuits, can and ought to be advanced through R.E. lessons. Equally all the skills necessary to engage in the art of extensive investigation, effective communication and rewarding relationships, can be developed and refined in the context of R.E. lessons. However, along with these general attitudinal and skill objectives, teachers of R.E. need to formulate objectives which are specific to particular units if not lessons, and consistent with the aims of the subject. To achieve this we adopt the following three categories of unit objectives:

Knowing

Every R.E. unit of work seeks to communicate to pupils (or rather to help them to discover), an important body of knowledge which arises out of the subject's extensive and complex field of enquiry. This is material which the pupils can learn, and, at an appropriate time and in an appropriate manner, recall and express. Ideally each unit should help pupils assimilate new knowledge and/or reinforce previously acquired knowledge.

TABLE 7 Plan for a unit of work

RELIGIOUS EDUCATION

School: _____

Age range: _____   Approach: Systems/Life Themes _____

Topic: _____

Content overview: _____
_____
_____
_____
_____
_____

Objectives: Knowing: _____
_____
_____

Understanding: _____
_____
_____

Reflecting: _____
_____
_____

Activities: _____
_____
_____
_____
_____
_____
_____
_____
_____
_____
_____
_____
_____

Resources: _____
_____
_____
_____

Assessment: _____
_____
_____

Understanding

These kinds of objectives focus on ideas and concepts and the complex relationship between them and isolated items of knowledge. They are concerned with promoting the pupil's appreciation of deeper meanings, and their understanding of the relative significance of difficult items of knowledge which they may glean about the subject under investigation.

Reflecting

At the heart of this subject is the human need to formulate or acquire a set of beliefs and values. The process by which individuals and groups acquire such beliefs and values is extremely complex. As already indicated it is not the role of R.E. in schools to prescribe what any individual's pattern of belief and behaviour will be. It is its task to help pupils to reflect, at a deeply personal level, on all the different beliefs and values, including their own, which are made available for exploration. Reflecting in this context means to evaluate in an honest and informed way, the worth and relevance of particular beliefs and values and the behaviour patterns which are likely to accompany them.

The balance of these three broad objectives will vary from age group to age group. In some cases there will be more emphasis on acquiring and organising new knowledge; in others the prime concern will be to extend understanding, while at other times the clear intention will be to encourage pupils to reflect on the beliefs, values and attitudes being explored.

Activities

Here the word activities refers to all those things which teachers and pupils do in the context of a school lesson which further the objectives. Of course, many other things which teachers and pupils do in the course of any given lesson are not directly related to subject and lesson objectives. They may be of a management, pastoral or disciplinary kind. Whether they are planned, intentional, or spontaneous, they are all part and parcel of teaching.

However, at this planning level we are concerned with identifying a large number of activities which teachers can use in different ways and situations to achieve some or all of the three kinds of unit objectives described above.

At the unit stage of planning, it is probably best to include as wide a range as possible of potential activities so that the unit is not tied to any one year or group of children. Setting out activities for units of work is an exercise to help the teacher to think round some of the different ways in which the topic may be explored. The activities need not be in any order or have a logical connection between them. At a later stage, in the sequencing of activities for lessons, the teacher will need to select the most suitable ones and arrange them in a teachable sequence. A further advantage in setting out activities in this way at the stage of unit planning is that other teachers can make use of the suggestions, at the same time using their own judgement about selection and sequence.

When writing out these teaching/learning activities some of the following points may be borne in mind:

- Give a clear indication of the nature of the activity in the form of an instruction to the teacher.
- Indicate the kind of subject matter you intend to explore. Give examples.
- Suggest ways in which the classroom may be organised and arranged to promote interaction between children or to advance their understanding.

Clearly, all the activities need to reflect the needs, capabilities and comprehension levels of the children for whom the unit is intended. At this planning level it is also important to ensure that each activity is relatively self-contained and that there is more than one activity designed to achieve the same objective. This allows teachers to make choices in the light of their own circumstances.

By way of a brief checklist we offer here a summary of the kinds of activities which form the basic media through which pupils get access to and acquire some share of human knowledge, understanding and experience. Skilled teachers of R.E. will include all of these in their teaching repertoire.

acting	playing
dancing	reading
drawing	recording
filming	singing
listening	smelling
looking	talking
making	tasting
miming	writing
painting	

Resources

The teacher's task in the classroom may be described as 'prismatic' – it is to draw together and select from the great wealth of human experience a very limited number of examples and to focus attention on them sharply. The world 'out there' has to be brought into the classroom for children to explore. Teaching resources are the means through which this is done.

The structure of this manual throughout has been deductive, starting from principles and working down to practicalities. This is, of course, not the practical way in which many – maybe most – teachers work. The choice of resources is a case in point. Ideally, resources should be chosen in order to meet objectives, not vice versa. In practice, a 'good' resource becomes available and a teacher plans a unit of work around it. Clearly, there has to be a compromise, because the ideal resources are rarely available, and in any case there are no resource items which are absolutely indispensable to R.E. The basic principle, however, in selecting resources is that they must further the objectives and genuinely contribute to learning.

Much of the subject matter of R.E. can only be made available in the classroom through the use of a variety of resources such as

  books (class sets or single copies for reference)
  charts and maps (normally for display)
  pictures and posters (large format for display, small for group work)
  audio-cassettes
  slides and filmstrips
  artefacts (including ritual objects, dress, food etc.)
  video
  computer software

To these must be added a range of materials for writing, drawing and modelling, filming etc.

Along with these inanimate resources, teachers of R.E. have an even more important, though understandably less used, set of human resources. Our earlier discussion on the field of enquiry stressed the important role of teacher's and children's own individual patterns of belief and behaviour as a potential source of content. Although these are always present in the classroom it is not always appropriate and easy to make them explicit and thus use them as subject matter for a particular lesson. Another obvious and highly valuable human resource may be found among other members of staff and members of local communities.

Again, important though these are, practical considerations and the inability of many people to articulate their beliefs and experiences in front of children make it difficult to use this pool of local resources. Nevertheless, an awareness of the difficulties should not prevent the imaginative and keen teacher from using such people sparingly and with sensitivity. When they are used, either in the classroom or at a place away from the school, it is important that teachers retain the management initiative and control. The visitor, as visitor, is a resource and not a replacement teacher. It is the teacher's professional responsibility to ensure that appropriate learning is taking place in accordance with the unit objectives.

Reference to resources at this stage of planning units should be specific. Where necessary there should be some indication of which resource item is recommended for use with particular activities.

Assessment
Every unit of work should include an opportunity for formal assessment and several opportunities for informal assessment. Any occasion where expressive work is done is an opportunity for assessment. The assessment should, as far as possible, test the objectives.

An example of a unit of work designed for the upper primary school

Approach: Systems

Topic: Jewish food laws

Content overview Regulations about kashrut are important to any understanding of Judaism, even though there is some variation in the strictness with which they are observed. Kashrut laws help to focus attention on the way in which the observance of rules is an important mark of Jewish identity, and on the way in which the home (the main focus of the rules) plays a key role in Jewish tradition. The context of this unit will therefore be the Jewish home. A consideration of these rules helps to build up an awareness of those aspects of life to which Jewish people attach importance.

Children in this age group are at a stage where information gathering and organising come most easily to them. They should therefore be able to explore the main details of the food laws and the way a Jewish family observes them. The extension of their basic knowledge will be the main emphasis of this unit.

This unit might form one in a series looking at Jewish practices, so that children are gradually building up their basic knowledge of Judaism.

Objectives
Knowing
  the word 'kosher' and its meaning
  the identity of permitted and prohibited foods
  the rule governing the separation of milk and meat products
  rules about the preparation of meat

the way the kitchen in an orthodox Jewish home is organised

Understanding
how food and meals have a special importance in the Jewish tradition
why it is important for many Jewish people to keep to the details of the rules

Reflecting
on the special care and thought given to the preparation of food
on the belief that God requires these rules to be observed

Activities
For example
Invite a Jewish mother into the class to talk about her home and explain why preparing food and meals is so important to her family. Have the children prepare some questions.
Show the children pictures of a kitchen in a Jewish home. Draw attention to important features, e.g. separate places for milk and meat cutlery.
Display the word 'kosher' prominently on the classroom wall. Have the children draw pictures giving examples of kosher foods and mount these on the wall.
Talk to the children about the rules for preparing meat. Have the children look up dietary laws in Deuteronomy 14 and Leviticus 11. Discuss with them why these rules may have been made.
Have the children write down some things they do not eat, and explain why; ask them if they think there is any difference between their reasons and the reasons Jewish people may give.

Resources
For example
● poster showing forbidden foods
● slides of Jewish home/kitchen
● copied extracts from Torah
● coloured paper, scissors, glue

Assessment
In class:
Get the children to talk about why they think a Jewish family might enjoy their mealtimes.

For homework:
The children are to imagine they are Jewish parents. They have to explain in writing to a young child in the family why they cannot eat

some of the tasty-looking things that their friends at school eat.

An example of a unit of work designed for the upper secondary school

Approach: Life Themes

Topic: Attitudes to poverty

Content overview Poverty is one of the key issues in shared human experience through which ultimate questions about human dignity and value can be raised most clearly. It is an area of the greatest relevance to young people growing up in the modern world.

By this stage, adolescents should be able to build on knowledge and understanding of this issue gained earlier in R.E. and in other subject areas, and on their awareness derived from the media.

There should not therefore be much need to go into detail on the causes of poverty or to examine particular situations or some of the political and economic solutions, except where they raise ultimate questions and moral issues. The focus of the unit is clearly on attitudes. There does need to be an awareness of the distinction between absolute and relative poverty, and between enforced and voluntary poverty. The unit will emphasise an understanding of the issues and help to raise questions in the students' minds about people's responses – including their own. This unit will form part of a series of units which explores issues and beliefs.

Objectives
Knowing
the difference between absolute and relative poverty
the difference between enforced and voluntary poverty
several examples of attitudes towards poverty

Understanding
some of the beliefs that underlie the attitudes
some of the moral questions that are raised by these attitudes

Reflecting
on what it means to be poor
on the belief that we all share responsibility for each other/belong to each other
on our own attitudes to poverty

Activities
For example
Have the students make two lists, one setting out what they think are essential needs and the other setting out what they think are luxuries. Get them to compare these lists in groups. Try to arrive at a consensus of five basic needs.

Have each student prepare a questionnaire to put to their peers/staff/relatives on their attitudes to poverty.

Remind students, briefly, of some of the factors which contribute to poverty, e.g. climate, sanitation, conflict, corruption.

Show an audiovisual programme which illustrates differing religious attitudes to, and beliefs about, the causes and cures of poverty, e.g. *Girl in Brazil* (B.B.C. Scene).

Distribute information about Christian Aid, e.g. 'Why Christian Aid?' and 'Christian Aid today'. Pupils working in small groups identify and list some of the key beliefs about poverty expressed in these documents.

Have the students carry out some research into Muslim teaching about zakat and attitudes to wealth and poverty.

Set up a debate on the motion that 'Earth has enough for every man's need but not every man's greed (Gandhi)'.

Invite a Christian nun to speak to the class about her vow of poverty.

Resources
- Wall chart showing some basic causes of poverty
- CAFOD project pack 'People in Brazil'
- B.B.C. Scene series (B.B.C. Television for schools) – *Girl in Brazil*
- Christian Aid information packs

Assessment
For example, have the students design a poster or collage expressing their own attitude to poverty.

2 Preparing lessons from units of work

Preparing lessons is, of course, a basic and continual task for teachers. As this is a manual intended primarily to help practising professional teachers improve their performance in relation to R.E., an understanding of the basic skills of teaching is taken for granted.

It may be helpful, however, for even the most experienced teacher to reflect again on some essential elements of the task of preparing R.E. lessons in the light of the contemporary nature of the subject. The following are worthy of consideration.

Lesson segments
Traditionally the shape of an R.E. lesson has been the presentation of material by the teacher followed by some form of pupil expression work, note-taking and discussion. The emphasis was on teacher input with a minimal amount of pupil participation in the discovery or generation of significant amounts of the content of the lesson.

In stressing the inclusion of activities when designing units, we have pointed to an additional, if not alternative shape. The lesson can be planned as a series of segments or activities which focus on a central topic and contribute in different ways to the achievement of the unit aims.

While in most cases each segment will have a natural and logical relationship with both the one that precedes it and the one that follows, this will not always be the case. On some occasions there can be within the one lesson an abrupt and complete change in style – for example, some unexpected happening in the classroom or elsewhere which the teacher is able to use to better advantage than continuing with the planned activity. Such abrupt changes can also be planned to show that the topic can be explored in different ways and from quite different perspectives. Deeper levels of understanding and reflection often result from such changes in activity styles.

The number of segments and the length of each segment within any given lesson will be determined by many factors. More important among them are the time available, the extent of the pupils' attention spans and the nature of the activity itself. For example, a finger painting segment with infant children may take more time than the telling of a story to the same group; a brainstorm session in an upper secondary class round the problems of violence will be much shorter than a formal debate about the value of pacifist beliefs or stances within different world religions.

Sequencing segments in a lesson

There is seldom any one right order in which to arrange the segments of a lesson once they have been selected. Here again teachers have to use their own professional judgement in the light of their immediate circumstances and their perception of the needs, interests and abilities of the pupils.

Alongside considerations of time and the logic of the subject matter, teachers should also take account of other roles that different activities can play in promoting and furthering the learning process. Depending very largely on where it comes in a lesson, an activity may be used to open up a topic, to encourage pupil participation and feedback, to develop understanding and to reinforce what has been covered previously.

The need to motivate

As all teachers know only too well, every child entering the classroom is not necessarily ready or willing to engage in the learning planned. The art of good teaching certainly includes the ability to capture the attention of at least the majority of the class and then to focus that attention on the subject at hand.

Activities designed to achieve this motivating purpose clearly come at the beginning of a lesson. There will be occasions however when some kind of attention-restoring activity is necessary at other points in the lesson. This is especially so with very young children and in lessons which occupy a rather long period of time.

In the context of R.E. it is also worth remembering that a great deal of the subject's content is interesting and may be already important to children. Providing them with a ready access to more information and with clear guidelines as to how they might explore the subject further, and express their responses to it, can often be highly motivating. The teacher does not always have to resort to gimmicky, amusing or disciplinary techniques in order to capture and retain pupils' attention.

The need to explore

A great deal has been said throughout this manual about the extensiveness and complexity of the R.E. field of enquiry. With such an enormous amount of interesting and challenging material to explore, it is surprising to discover that many pupils often describe its treatment in schools as boring, repetitive and irrelevant. Not all the blame for this can be laid at the teacher's door. Many very powerful influences are at work in the pupils' homes, among their peers and in society generally to reinforce such attitudes; but there is also evidence that when pupils are helped in imaginative ways to explore the mysteries, questions, beliefs, experiences and practices associated with religions in an open, informed and non-dogmatic way, they are capable of sustained intellectual enquiry and emotional involvement.

To achieve this, teachers need to select activities which provide pupils with opportunities to expand their knowledge and deepen their understanding of the subject's total field of enquiry. There is no excuse for an R.E. programme in schools which pupils can honestly describe as repeating the same old things year after year. No one using this manual will have reached this point without getting the clear message that the subject can be planned in a developmental way so that pupils know that they are exploring new material in increasingly demanding ways.

Teachers can be well satisfied if a significant number of their pupils leave their classes making such comments as 'I never knew that before' or 'That is the first time that I have really understood what X is all about'. As pointed out above, this kind of response is in itself motivation for further exploration and discovery. One lesson's exploration activities may well provide another lesson with its motivation segment.

The need to express

A great deal has been said so far about the nature of contemporary R.E. and the ways in which it can be approached and structured to achieve its general aim. This in turn demands of teachers that they provide ample scope for pupils to express, through a variety of media, their own beliefs and values and the relationship which these may have to those traditional belief systems being explored in the R.E. programme.

If, as we have claimed, the aim of R.E. is to help pupils mature in relation to their own individual pattern of belief, then an increasing ability to identify and articulate how and why they differ from alternative commitments would seem to be an essential skill to be acquired. The aims and objectives of the subject require lesson activities which provide opportunities for pupil expression.

Implicit in such an aim is a further claim that the pupil's present pattern of belief, however immature, confused or ill-informed, is a potential source of content. This potential content can only become available for exploration and evaluation if and when it is given coherent expression in the classroom. While teachers cannot plan in advance to use such content on any given occasion, they can design activities which provide maximum opportunity and freedom for pupils to give expression to their own ideas and their responses to the range of beliefs being explored.

Anyone familiar with the major world religions will know that deeply held beliefs and convictions are not adequately expressed simply in descriptive prose or through the language and concepts of historical or scientific investigation and discourse. The whole range of expressive and imaginative forms of communication is used and R.E., if it is to be true to its subject matter and aims, must advance pupils' skills in relation to their use. Just as the belief systems have, since they began, expressed themselves through art, music, story, poetry, ritual, symbol and drama, so must R.E. lessons provide pupils with regular opportunities to express their beliefs and ideas through these different media.

If a further case for the inclusion of expressive activities in R.E. were needed, it is surely to be found in the important teaching task of pupil assessment and feedback. The effectiveness of each of the types of assessment (diagnostic, formative and summative) is almost entirely dependent on the pupils' ability to express themselves clearly and with increasing sophistication. (See Part Five.)

To reiterate, there is no one set pattern or sequence of activities for all R.E. lessons. Teachers will find their own style for planning lessons which, on most occasions combine segments which motivate pupils and help them to explore and express faith responses.

3 Organisation in the classroom

Here we are concerned mainly with the range of different groupings of pupils which seem possible, desirable and practical when preparing and presenting R.E. lessons. An understanding of these ought to contribute to a more efficient management of the programme whether it takes place in a traditional or multiple area type of school; whether it is a primary, middle or secondary school. A willingness and ability to use a variety of physical arrangements in the classroom can provide scope for a greater range of teaching activities and therefore learning experiences for pupils.

A large group

In this case the class or year group is kept in one large group and all pupils attend to the same activity. This will usually be in the form of direct teacher input, e.g. lecturing, telling, demonstrating, story-telling, questioning or audiovisual presentation.

| The whole class or group together |

Medium-sized groups

Pupils are arranged in a number of medium-sized groups, with perhaps five to ten pupils in a group. Some may be directly taught, especially if a team-teaching situation exists; other may be engaged in some form of self-directed work, e.g. discussion, research, project work or planning.

Small groups

On these occasions two to five pupils are working together, usually on a specific task set by the teacher or selected from a series of electives. This can be a useful management device in mixed ability classes, provided that there are sufficient resources available to support the range of activities prepared.

Individual work

The emphasis here is more on how the pupils are working rather than on any physical arrangement. Provided that conditions are conducive to the kind of activity and work expected, the actual classroom arrangements are less significant.

INDIVIDUAL PUPILS

Clearly these components can be arranged in very many different ways. Part of the teacher's task in planning to capture and maintain pupils' interest lies in varying the pattern so that the situation is not too often repeated, or so that pupils are not required to spend too long in any one situation.

Two further symbols may be used to indicate teacher/pupil interaction:

A triangle with its apex above the base line can be used to show when the teacher is directly addressing the group.

A triangle pointing downwards indicates a situation where pupils report back on their work or direct questions to the teacher.

By combining these symbols we may present diagrammatically a number of possible patterns of pupil arrangement, which teachers can use and thus again expand their teaching repertoire.

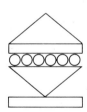

This is a fairly standard pattern. The teacher introduces the topic to the whole class, who then divide into medium-sized groups for discussion. Towards the end of the time, the groups report back to the whole of the class.

This is another familiar pattern. After the general introduction, pupils, either individually or in small groups, get on with their work. Feedback is directly to the teacher(s) and not to the whole class.

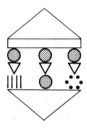

This is a slightly more complex structure possibly requiring a longer period of time. After the introduction, pupils are set in three medium-sized groups. These report progress to the teacher who then sets further work, either for individuals, the larger group, or small groups. Final reporting or presentation is to the whole class.

We are indebted to Professor S. Markland of Scandinavia for the idea of using these symbols in this way.

4 Presenting religious matters in the classroom

The concern here is not about the nature and function of so-called 'religious language'. It is to do with ways of talking about and presenting religious matters in an open educational context.

Most experienced teachers are well aware of the need to use words that are meaningful to pupils. For example it is not helpful to use technical religious terms unless their meaning is explained, or to use terms which are beyond the present experience or comprehension level of the pupils. Similarly, difficulties in communication arise when terms which have multiple meanings or have a range of associations are used without detailed explanation. Words like 'meek' and 'father', important within the Christian tradition, may be understood in very different ways depending on their accepted usage among people with whom pupils live and perhaps on the experiences that pupils have had. Terms which produce positive feelings in some people may have negative meanings for others.

However there are a few other language styles and conventions which are required of teachers when they are presenting religious matters within the context of R.E. A failure to adopt and maintain these conventions often results in both a breakdown in communication and in increasing resentment on the part of many pupils.

While these conventions are essential to the purposes of R.E., they are not unique to it. They are in fact used by most adults when they engage in conversation with others about controversial issues. These are accepted protocols and manners which are used to avoid any appearance of pushing one's own ideas and beliefs 'down someone else's throat'. Adults exercising these protocols endeavour to show respect for each other's views while at the same time taking the opportunity to voice, strongly if need be, personally held convictions.

In order to make clear the nature of these conventions and to stress their importance for R.E., we introduce the notion of 'owning and grounding'.

Owning and grounding

Central to this need to own or ground belief statements is the distinction between 'fact' and 'belief' types of statement. Among other things, such statements are those about which differences of outlook are found within the community. Particularly in R.E., they include statements about God, claims about religious leaders or interpretations of sacred books. For example, in speaking about Jesus, a distinction may be made between saying that he was crucified at a particular time or place and saying that he was the Christ who died for the sins of the whole world in accordance with God's plan. The first statement could be the factual reporting of any observer and is potentially open to historical research. The latter statement presumes a belief about who Jesus was and thus is of a different kind.

It is possible, indeed it is essential to the purposes of R.E., that both kinds of statements be used in the classroom and that pupils become aware of the distinction between them and skilled in using them appropriately.

Sometimes teachers and pupils may own a particular belief as theirs, by the use of such terms as 'I believe...', 'It seems to me that...', 'I feel...', 'I think...', or 'In my experience...'.

Alternatively they may ground the belief by attaching it to some groups of people who hold it, or to some source from which it comes, for example, 'Muslims believe...', or 'It says in the Qur'an...', or 'Some/many people do not believe...'.

Owning or grounding a belief does not prove or assume that it is true or authoritative for others. However, because it does not presume upon their agreement the pupils are more likely to be able to hear and to discuss what is being presented and may not feel that particular beliefs or values are being forced on them.

When beliefs are owned or grounded they sound less dogmatic, and some may fear they will sound less authoritative. However, when the source of their authority, whether in personal experience or in a tradition, is made clear, this provides important data for those who are being asked to consider where they stand in relation to those beliefs. A quick way to check the authority or source of a belief statement is to ask 'Who says it?' or 'Who believes it?' This assists teachers and/or pupils either to own the statement or to ground it by indicating who believes it to be true.

Several benefits can be seen to follow when belief statements are either owned or grounded:

1 Teachers have greater freedom to deal with their own beliefs in class.

2 Conversation about beliefs becomes more open and easier to develop, in that once teachers and pupils learn either to own or to ground statements of belief, it is easier for others to respond with their beliefs, whether these are the same or different.

3 By this approach teachers do not presume upon the beliefs of their pupils, so helping to avoid the negative reactions and discipline problems that such presumption can generate.

4 Most religions acknowledge the importance of faith decisions as part of the development of religious maturity. However, when beliefs are referred to as if everyone thinks that way, the role of decision is hidden. In contrast, if beliefs are owned or grounded the issue is brought into the open for consideration. In this way pupils can become aware of the importance of these decisions, without any implication of an attempt to enforce or require commitment to a particular belief.

5 Some pupils are placed in a situation of tension when they receive contradictory views on belief issues from various significant adults. The language of teachers can heighten this tension or it can support and encourage the pupils in working out their own patterns of belief. If these conventions of owning and grounding are maintained from the earliest primary school years, pupils may be better prepared to work through the faith struggles which often characterise the teenage years.

6 One of the difficulties facing teachers of R.E. is that of making the content as concrete as possible. When beliefs are owned or grounded they are linked to individuals or groups who hold them. This will help to make them more concrete in that the beliefs are seen as having implications for people's lives.

7 When referring to sacred writings, care in owning and grounding can help clarify the way in which they are being used. This will involve distinguishing between (i) quotations (ii) interpretations or summary statements based on someone's reading of the text and (iii) implicit claims concerning the authority of the book in people's lives. For example, the statement 'The Guru Granth Sahib says...' is a form of grounding if it can be followed by the question 'Where does it say it?'

8 Owning or grounding their references to beliefs can help teachers communicate more easily. It enables them to speak in a way that is inclusive of all pupils, without making assumptions about prior commitments. It also provides an example which can assist the pupils in giving clearer expression to their own beliefs and attitudes.

PART FIVE

HOW CAN R.E. BE ASSESSED?

The basic premise of this Part is that assessment of the work of children is as important in Religious Education as in any other area of the curriculum. Since we are dealing with a subject which claims the same basis in education as any other subject, we shall need to follow the same educational principles. One of these is that assessment is an essential part of the learning process. Without some form of assessment we cannot discover the level of understanding which children already have, whether children are making progress or what they may have learned as a result of our teaching. Moreover, the point that will be stressed in this Part is that assessment is itself one of the means by which children learn.

There have been in the past, and still are in many schools, a number of serious difficulties which impede the carrying out of useful assessment in this subject. Some of these difficulties arise from uncertainty in the minds of some teachers about what we are actually assessing in R.E. We are assessing the development of children's understanding about religion and their own personal response to it. In other words we are assessing the extent to which pupils gradually increase their knowledge and understanding of what this manual calls the R.E. field of enquiry. We are also assessing pupils' willingness and ability to reflect on the issues, questions and experiences which emerge from it.

There are, however, some obvious difficulties in assessing, in any formal way, the early development of understanding in very young children in the primary school. The emphasis here will be on those more informal and intuitive assessments which teachers of young primary children are making all the time. Discussions with individual children, listening to their conversations and encouraging their self-expression, will all provide pointers to the children's development in this area of the curriculum. Since it will not be either possible or desirable to draw distinctive subject boundaries in the work they are doing, the assessments will obviously be more wide-ranging than those simply limited to an assessment of children's understanding of religion. Nonetheless, whether formally or informally, assessment will be an integral part of children's learning and of the teacher's awareness of progress and development.

Other difficulties arise from practical considerations, particularly those of the timetable in the secondary school. Where one teacher is asked to teach a subject to virtually every child for one thirty-five minute period each week, it is almost impossible to carry out any meaningful assessment of the progress of individual children. About the only achievable goals in this situation are that every child should know the teacher's name and subject title by half way through the school year, and that the teacher should know at least half the children's names by the end of it. Any regular testing and recording of children's progress is wholly impracticable, and teachers should not be put in the position where they are expected to do this.

Meaningful assessment can only be carried out where there is adequate provision on the timetable for the teaching of the subject. Those who face the difficulties outlined above may well be best advised to react by refusing to be drawn into the obsession – created by some teachers, parents and children – with endless grading of individual work on a competitive basis, and concentrate on group or class assessment on a more cooperative basis. For the nature of the subject is such that it is less concerned with measuring individual gradings than with the way in which children are learning from it, especially in interaction with each other, and the benefits they are deriving from it in terms of personal growth and maturity.

The exercise of assessment depends entirely on the goals or objectives that a teacher sets out to achieve. Assessment is therefore concerned with measuring the extent to which those objectives have been achieved. Objectives can be set at various levels, ranging from the total school programme down to individual lessons. They require the most careful thought to ensure that they are realistic, attainable and, as far as possible, assessable. This manual does not deal in detail with objectives at every level, but examples of unit objectives are given as illustrations in Part Four.

1 Purposes of assessment

Broadly speaking the purposes of assessment may be divided into three areas. These are:

A **Diagnostic** – Finding out the level of understanding children have at the beginning of a course.

B **Formative** – Helping to reinforce what they are learning.

C **Summative** – Finding out what they have learned at the end of a course and, where necessary, putting them into grades.

DIAGNOSTIC

At the beginning of any long course of work – such as the start of a year, or the move from primary to secondary school, or where a new teacher takes over – it is important to know where the children are starting from, and what level of knowledge and understanding they bring to the course. This information will help the teacher in planning the course and in deciding on the ground that needs to be covered. This is particularly pertinent at the start of secondary schooling, where children normally come from a range of feeder primary schools in which the level of development of religious understanding may be varied. There is also a strong argument for closer liaison between primary and secondary schools – a feature which is essential to the kind of developmental R.E. envisaged in this manual.

Diagnostic assessment is necessarily broad. It will

TABLE 8 **Questions which could be used as a basis for a diagnostic test**

Are children aware of diversity in religious belief and practice?

Are they willing to explore the beliefs and practices of others in an open way?

Do they have more than a formal knowledge of acts about religions?

In particular, have they begun to explore the 'hidden' elements of belief, value and spirituality?

Are they able to discern the way in which language is used by religions in a metaphorical and parabolic way?

Do they have an understanding of what symbols and myths are for?

Are they able to recognise a moral issue?

Are they able to recognise an ultimate question?

Are they able to hold a discussion on a controversial issue in a tolerant and frank way?

Do they have anything more than a formal understanding of concepts such as 'God' or 'faith'?

range over wide areas and cover as much ground as possible. It is not really concerned with specific details, but with general knowledge and understanding. If a first-year secondary teacher is proposing to start the year by looking at some general questions about religion, the teacher will want to know something about the understanding that the children already have. There is no need to explore the wealth of detailed information that the children may or may not have acquired, though there are some very basic items of factual knowledge about religion that children ought to know before they leave the primary school.

It is also necessary for the secondary teacher to bear in mind that the appearance of the R.E. dimension in the primary school may be quite different from that which dominates in the secondary school; for example, children may have no real perception of R.E. as a separate subject. Thus the forms of diagnostic testing used must reflect an integrated approach and allow each child to draw on examples from a variety of different religions, since it is unlikely that they will have covered precisely the same traditions in exactly the same way.

Any diagnostic test will, therefore, need to explore children's general awareness and understanding with great flexibility in regard to the use of the particular examples used.

Table 8 (page 63) sets out a range of general areas of understanding which teachers in lower secondary classes will need to assess before they can plan appropriate programmes of R.E. for pupils entering their schools. Of course, the closer the liaison between secondary schools and their feeder primary schools, the easier it is to ensure that the curricula in both schools are designed to achieve this kind of progressive learning in regard to R.E.

FORMATIVE

For the purposes of R.E. this is the most important element in assessment. It is designed to help children in the learning process and to assist them towards mastering an understanding of the subject. Regular testing (by a variety of techniques) is one of the ways of reinforcing learning. When children have explored a particular topic, their understanding of it and the knowledge they have gained can actually be strengthened and deepened by this form of assessment. It also provides a guideline for the teacher who wants to know how much progress children have made in meeting the set objectives. Formative assessment is related to short units of work and takes place at frequent intervals.

Formative assessment is concerned with very specific objectives over a relatively short period of time. It will therefore be used to assess matters of detail related to a specific unit of work. It should elicit evidence about how far children have taken in the information they have been dealing with, and how far they have understood it. At the same time, the teacher will use this opportunity also to observe how far children are continuing to use some of the basic principles of the subject they have already learned. For example, whether in a class discussion they are able to wait their turn or disagree without shouting, or whether, in an exercise in picture analysis, they show imagination in the questions they ask.

Since we are concerned here with using assessment actually to reinforce learning, it follows that this aim will only be achieved if children are given the maximum opportunity to learn from the assessment. This means that feedback is essential. The feedback, however, is *not* for comparative or competitive purposes ('How many have I got right?') but to further the learning process. In other words, it should help the child to identify errors or false assumptions and to ask questions about them in order to clarify them. It can also help the teacher to make decisions about whether to go over a piece of work again, or whether to introduce more detailed and varied examples to illustrate a concept – or whether the exploration can be taken to a deeper level because the children have quickly grasped the issues.

SUMMATIVE

This area covers those assessment procedures which take place towards the end of a course of work. Such a 'course' may be of a short, medium or long-term duration: a few weeks, a term, a year or longer. The important point is that the particular area of study is, in a formal teaching sense, at an end. Within the context of the school programme, pupils know that they will not be expected to recall, under test conditions, material dealt with in this particular section of study. They will also know that the test could be both broad and specific. It will cover all the objectives of the course and range over the whole unit and perhaps syllabus. It will be specific in the sense that the assessment will use detailed examples as a basis for testing. It will test whether a child is able to apply basic learning to both familiar and unfamiliar examples.

Summative test instruments may be devised, administered and marked by people outside the school or by the teachers who have been directly involved in the teaching of the pupils being assessed. In both cases, namely, external examinations or school-based assessment, some form of moderation needs to be established to ensure a high degree of comparability in terms of levels of difficulty and marking schemes.

Over recent years many forms of continuous assessment have emerged. Pupils' work submitted over a period of time is assessed and scores are accumulated to provide an accurate picture of their levels of performance in relation to the course objectives. A single written test, under examination conditions on a particular day, is not the only way of determining pupil abilities either in relation to academic criteria or in relation to one another.

Clearly the amount and style of feedback that pupils receive from summative tests, depends on which of the above kinds of testing is being used. With external 'final' examinations, the amount of feedback is minimal. In the case of public examinations this will be little more than the reporting of grades and the award of certificates. With school-based continuous assessment, feedback can be more substantial and indeed play both a summative and a formative role in the child's continuing education.

2 Techniques of assessment

The techniques we use for assessment are the actual means by which we test children. It is most important to bear in mind that there are available to us a wide range of techniques, and that it is a mistake to equate assessment simply with written tests. The basic principle is that assessment can take place whenever children demonstrate the kind of behaviour envisaged in the objectives which the teacher has set. Thus a whole range of tasks can be given to children at any time, through which the teacher can carry out assessment, sometimes in an informal way, at others in a much more structured or formal context.

INFORMAL ASSESSMENT

Just to remind ourselves that assessment is not the same as a test, we should recall how as teachers many of the indicators of children's progress we pick up are those which arise from informal situations. This is particularly the case in R.E., where the development of understanding and the capacity to reflect are given a high priority.

There is a sense in which formative assessment is taking place whenever a teacher listens to what children are saying informally, whether this is in a private discussion between the teacher and the child, or in a broader discussion or debate. Listening to a group of children who have been asked to discuss a particular topic may be very revealing in terms of what the children really understand, and may suggest to the teacher the need to reinforce a particular point at some later stage.

The assessment of informal oral expression in an individual, group or class context is a key area in R.E. where the interaction of children and the ways in which they respond to each other in relation to their ideas, beliefs, values and attitudes is of the greatest importance in helping them in their personal and social development.

FORMAL ASSESSMENT

This takes place whenever teachers decide to give children a task in which they are being tested in relation to set objectives. Variety is once again the key to the exercise. Some techniques of assessment are better suited to particular objectives. Here we simply illustrate some of the techniques which can be used. Table 9 (page 66) should be read in conjunction with the following notes. It provides some concrete examples of the various assessment techniques which might be applied to a class of middle school pupils after their visit to a mosque.

Oral tests
These are particularly useful when a teacher wants a general impression of how much a class of children have actually learned and understood. A few quick questions are asked of individuals in the class relating to the material being studied. Further, more exploratory questions are then asked which become

TABLE 9 **Formal assessment techniques applied to a group of middle school pupils' visit to a mosque** In order to gain a balanced view of assessment techniques, Table 10 should also be referred to.	
Assessment technique	Example of how to test
Oral tests	*Quick questions* What is the tall tower outside the mosque for? Why do they have a special washing place in the mosque? *Exploratory questions* Why do you think it is important that everything is so clean? What do you think the people feel when they bow right down to the ground?
Written tests	*Gap-filling exercises* 'Outside the mosque we saw a tower called a .... From the top of this in Muslim countries, a man calls the people to tell them it is time for......... . When people come to the mosque, they take off their ...., then they wash their ...., ... and .... Inside the mosque the people face towards the .... which points in the direction of the .... in Mecca.' *One word or short paragraph answers* What name or title is given to the man who leads the prayers in a mosque? What is a minaret? Why are there clocks on the wall of the mosque pointing to different times? *Link-making exercises* At a simple level: Minaret Prayer leader Imam Prayer times Clocks Tower At a more difficult level: Washing Encouragement Prayer Purity Sermon Submission At a sophisticated level (not for middle school): Qur'an Discipline Allah Revelation Salat One-ness *Multiple-choice questions* Underline the words which give the best ending to this sentence. The imam is the person who – climbs the tower to call people to prayer. – is in charge of the mosque. – reads the Qur'an to himself. – leads the prayers in the mosque. – collects money from the visitors.

the basis for a discussion. By listening carefully to the answers, a teacher can learn how far the children have begun to understand the material under study. The children, too, are learning through the assessment. Of course, assessing children's learning in this way can only give general impressions about a group, rather than precise information about each individual.

Written tests

These would normally be used as a means of testing an individual child's level of knowledge and understanding, and may take many forms. Some techniques are useful for testing basic recall of factual knowledge:

Cloze procedure

A teacher sets out a passage of writing from which certain key words or phrases have been omitted.

Since exercises such as these are looking for clear, objective answers, teachers need to take care that the meaning is absolutely clear and that only one answer is really possible.

Where there is a possibility of more than one answer, the teacher needs to phrase the exercise so that it gives a clear lead. This involves anticipating the way children may see the task as well as what the teacher requires.

One word or short paragraph answers

These questions can be answered in one word or in very brief statements. They are useful for testing factual knowledge.

The same principles of clarity and precision apply here as with the cloze procedure.

Link making exercises

The teacher sets out two columns of words or phrases and asks children to link appropriate items with each other.

This can be used for testing factual knowledge, or it can be used to test an understanding of concepts.

Multiple choice questions

This is another exercise in which information is provided, but children have a choice, and have to make a correct identification.

To be a useful exercise, there does need to be a real element of choice in the answers given, so that the alternatives are not too obviously impossible. The task can be made quite difficult, and require a lot of thought, where the alternatives are closely related and where the best alternative is what is sought.

All these examples of formal assessment are fairly straightforward ways of testing basic knowledge,

comprehension and understanding. There are lots of other techniques that teachers use (such as crosswords, puzzles and other wordgames) which serve the same assessment purposes, and which provide variety for the children.

There are, of course, other more extended forms of written tests which can be used by teachers. These will involve children in writing about a particular aspect of the work they have done to show that they have thought about it and understood it. The teacher will have a good idea what to expect from the task that is set, and will therefore word that task as clearly as possible so that the children understand what they are to do.

They may, for example, be given an essay to write, and the teacher may supply a title for their work, e.g. 'Our visit to the mosque'. That is actually a very poor essay title, because while the teacher may be hoping for all sorts of interesting information and intelligent insight and perceptive impressions, the children are given very little clue what they are expected to write about, apart from a bald record of what they did and saw. It might be much better if the teacher gave some guidance as to what was expected, for example:

'The title is "Our visit to the mosque". When you write your essay, think about what we did and what we saw at the mosque. What sort of things did you find strange or interesting? Try and use some of the important words we learned, and say what they mean. And think about what you felt as you watched the men saying their prayers all together.'

The exercise is now more clearly structured, and opens the way for assessing not only the basic facts that children have learned, but what they have understood and how they have responded with their own feelings.

Essays need not be of great length. They can be as short as a paragraph or two. However, they do give an opportunity to children to show some understanding of what they are learning.

We might mention here one other related technique that can usefully be used in this context. This is the technique of giving children a number of related tasks which arise from a stimulus or focus that the teacher provides. It could be a picture of the inside of a mosque, or it could be a description written by someone else, or it could be a particular object, such as a prayer mat or a copy of the Qur'an. On the basis of one or more of these, a number of related questions could be asked which give children an opportunity to explore an aspect of their visit by focussing their attention on a significant stimulus.

Expressive and creative work

Although expressive work may often be in individual

written form, it is not necessarily always so. There is also a sense in which expressive work may be seen as an extension of the written or oral test, but a distinction may usefully be drawn. In the more formal tests we have so far considered, the teacher is looking for evidence of basic knowledge and understanding. With expressive work it is possible to take this a stage further, and use it to assess how far children's understanding can really take them and, most important of all, how much insight they have in expressing their own reactions to what they are learning about. In other words, assessing children's expressive and creative work focusses on the element of reflecting in the objectives of R.E.

This is an area of assessment that is not tied to any one technique but it may very usefully be explored in several ways. Table 10 should also be read in conjunction with the following notes as it provides examples of how expressive and creative work might be used to assess the visit to the mosque.

Creative writing in prose or poetry
This will tend to focus on children's reflections and experiences of what they have seen and done.

Art or modelling
Work of this kind could be used to highlight children's awareness of things they perceive to be important. This sort of work could be done individually or in groups.

Creative oral work and drama
The focus here is not simply on re-enacting something that has been seen, but on entering into the spirit of it. Groups might be asked to devise a role play, for instance, to show that they have grasped

TABLE 10 **Assessment through expressive and creative work of a group of middle school pupils' visit to a mosque**
In order to gain a balanced view of assessment techniques, Table 9 should also be referred to.

Assessment technique	Example of how to test
Creative work in prose and poetry	Pupils might be asked to think about and write about the strong feeling of brotherhood which the Muslims share e.g. their feeling of being together in prayer, or the warmth they show in their greetings and conversation; or pupils might think and write about their own feelings at being in the mosque, e.g. the spaciousness, the cleanliness, the colour.
Art or modelling	A group might be asked to depict visually how the mosque is a 'hive of activity'; to prepare a poster urging Muslim parents to send their children to Qur'an school.
Creative oral work and drama	Pupils might be put into a role-play situation then asked to enter into a discussion between leaders of the mosque and members of the local neighbourhood over the question of allowing the call to prayer to be publicly broadcast from the the newly-built minaret.

what the issues are all about, and what others may feel. A perceptive teacher could make some important assessments of how far the children really have understood the feelings and concerns of others.

In all this assessment of expressive and creative work, the emphasis of the teacher is two-fold. Firstly, it is on providing the necessary stimulus to get children really thinking creatively about what they are doing. Secondly, it is on encouraging the children to go on exploring, and on avoiding passing judgement in the sense of what may be regarded as 'right' and 'wrong' answers. Teachers are assessing how far children are thinking creatively and imaginatively about the subject and are being interested, engaged and thoughtful in their responses. If they are not doing these things, the subject is failing them.

Research assessment

A further area for formal assessment is the children's ability, on the basis of what they have learned, to carry out their own independent exploration of a topic. This provides an opportunity for the teacher to learn something about children's overall grasp of their work and of the principles of the subject. It also gives the teacher a chance to find out whether children have been sufficiently motivated to carry on their exploration beyond the classroom.

Homework is a very useful vehicle for providing this kind of assessment, but it can and perhaps should be part of the formal teaching/assessing procedures. It is a golden opportunity to take children's learning further, and should not be relegated to the level where children are told 'Finish off your work at home'.

Children in both primary and secondary schools can be helped to design, plan, carry out and report findings from research projects related to particular areas of the R.E. field of enquiry. Searching for information in libraries, interviewing people, classifying and recording findings in a variety of ways, presenting material through a range of different media are all part and parcel of school work and can be used to great effect in this subject.

Conclusion

None of the techniques of assessment is in any way exclusive to R.E. The nature of the subject does, however, suggest that a balance of more formal techniques and some of the informal ones will be the best way of furthering children's learning. It also demands that a high premium is placed on the teacher's assessment of children's creative, imaginative and expressive work, in order to ensure that the emphasis of the subject on the children's own development is clearly maintained.

3 Assessment through external examinations

We have no intention of entering here into the debate about the desirability or viability of public examinations as an educational exercise either in general or in relation to this subject.

External examinations do, however, play a significant part in the school curriculum. They have an undoubted influence on what is taught and how it is taught throughout the secondary school. As far as R.E. is concerned they are an important consideration in determining the status with which the subject is regarded in schools. This factor has negative implications as well as positive influences.

On the positive side the examinations can provide an identifiable goal towards which students can work in the final years of the secondary school. One of the more negative considerations is the question of whether Religious Education can be adequately assessed in an objective public examination which cannot, by its nature, really test some of those important affective and reflective aspects of the subject which are vital to it. That is why the

examination subject is usually referred to as Religious Studies, indicating that the examination is best suited to measuring students' level of cognitive understanding.

The external examination is a summative test for grading purposes. As such it should represent an assessment of the level of knowledge, understanding and evaluation that a child has in this case achieved by the age of leaving secondary school. It should, therefore, be a summative test in the sense that it draws together the threads of a child's growing understanding of the subject over the years of schooling.

THE GENERAL CERTIFICATE OF SECONDARY EDUCATION

The G.C.S.E. examinations, starting in the United Kingdom in 1988, provide a system for all children at the end of secondary education in which common aims, objectives and schemes of assessment are clearly stated for all subjects. The national criteria for Religious Studies state the aims and assessment objectives for this subject. These objectives are entirely in line and consistent with the kind of R.E. that has been worked out in this manual and courses for primary and secondary pupils based on the principles set out here will lead naturally to the G.C.S.E. examination.

It does seem entirely appropriate, if not essential, that the principles and procedures which shape the subject throughout the primary and secondary years, should also underpin the form of assessment which pupils face at sixteen plus. These principles and procedures are established in their own right as providing a necessary component of children's education, whether they take formal examinations or not. External formal examinations are only one important way of assessing the success of courses based on these principles and of pupils' performance in relation to the aims of the subject. The school-based coursework element, which is included in these new examinations, provides another means for testing some of the objectives of R.E. which have been enunciated in this manual.

For the sake of clarity and illustration the objectives from the national criteria are set out in Table II.

TABLE 11 **Extract from G.C.S.E. – the national criteria: Religious Studies**
(D.E.S. Welsh Office, H.M.S.O. 1985)

1 Introduction

1.1 These criteria state the essential requirements of all syllabuses bearing the subject title Religious Studies. They relate to GCSE examinations and do not in any way prescribe the aims, form or content of the total 11-16 curriculum for Religious Education.

1.2 All syllabuses and examinations should be open to candidates of any religious persuasion or none and should provide a broad structure for the study of religion, emphasising its educational basis.

2 Aims

The general aims of a course of study leading to GCSE examinations in Religious Studies should be

2.1 to promote an enquiring, critical and sympathetic approach to the study of religion, especially in its individual and corporate expression in the contemporary world;

2.2 to introduce candidates to the challenging and varied nature of religion and to the ways in which this is reflected in experience, belief and practice;

2.3 to help candidates to identify and explore questions about the meaning of life and to consider such questions in relation to religious traditions;

2.4 to encourage candidates to reflect on religious responses to moral issues;

2.5 to enable candidates to recognise and appreciate the contribution of religion in the formation of patterns of belief and behaviour.

3 Assessment objectives

The italicised notes are intended to illustrate the application of the objectives to examples of content. The illustrations are taken from a variety of religious traditions in order to demonstrate that the criteria are appropriate to the study of any religious tradition.

An examination shall test the extent to which candidates are able to

3.1 select and present relevant factual information in an organised manner;

3.2 show understanding of

3.2.1 language, terms and concepts used in religion;

Candidates may be expected to show that they are able to understand the various ways of conveying meaning in religion, for example poetry, metaphor, allegory, parable, myth, symbol; the application of particular terminology in religion, for example church, baptism, priest, and to recognise and use key religious concepts, for example faith, salvation, sacrament.

3.2.2 the role and importance in religion of special people, writings and traditions;

Candidates may be expected to show that they are aware of the ways in which the appeal to authority influences both individuals and religious communities in matters of faith and practice; and that authority may be exercised in a variety of forms, for example through religious leaders past or present, through sacred texts or through the community's tradition; thus the Papacy, the Bible and the Apostolic Tradition all represent in differing degrees and contexts sources of authority within the Christian Church.

3.2.3 principal beliefs of the religion or religions being studied, the meanings given to those beliefs by adherents and the ways in which beliefs are related to the personal and corporate practice of religion;

Candidates may be expected to show that they are able to give an account in outline of those religious beliefs which are fundamental to at least one major world religion (Buddhism, Christianity, Hinduism, Islam, Judaism, Sikhism shall be considered the major world religions for the purpose of defining content); to explain in simple language what those beliefs mean to believers; and to be aware, wherever appropriate, of some varieties of interpretation of those beliefs; for example, the Jewish faith is founded on the Torah; the follower of the Jewish faith seeks to apply the Law to every part of life, and strives to understand the most appropriate way to do so; not all agree about how precisely the Law should be applied to particular circumstances, and there is debate within the community to arrive at satisfactory answers on the basis of the study of the Law, of what earlier teachers have said and of the contemporary situation.

3.2.4 religious and, where appropriate, non-religious responses to contemporary moral issues, both personal and social;

Candidates may be expected to show that they understand something of the ways in which believers and religious communities respond to some significant moral issues; for example the problem of violence in the modern world may be related to the teaching of Buddhism about non-violence and ways in which Buddhists express their commitment to non-violence. It may be appropriate for candidates in this case to set alongside the Buddhist view the teaching of a secular ideology not opposed to the use of violence in order to understand more fully the distinctive elements of Buddhist teaching.

3.2.5 questions about the meaning of life and the variety of faith-responses which may be given to them;

Candidates may be expected to show that they are able to recognise those questions about life, its purpose and meaning, origins and destiny, to which responses of faith are given; that they understand that such responses are varied, yet lie at the root of religious belief and practice; for example study of Hindu belief in karma and samsara will help students to raise the whole question of whether there is life after death and to be aware of other responses to the same question.

3.3 evaluate, on the basis of evidence and argument, issues of belief and practice arising from the study of religion;

Candidates are encouraged not only to be aware of differences of opinion in matters of religious belief and practice, but also to express an opinion of their own, based on the use of evidence and argument at a simple level. In this case, it is the evaluative process that is being assessed. It cannot be emphasised too strongly that this element in the assessment objectives is in no way intended to test the validity of any viewpoint held by candidates, but only to assess the extent to which they are able to express and support an opinion coherently. In accordance with the principle that all examinations in Religious Studies are open to candidates of any religious persuasion or of none, questions, schemes of marking, etc. must in no way require of candidates a predetermined opinion which they may not share.

PART
SIX

SUMMARY

We began in the first Part of this book with a statement of a general aim for Religious Education. From this aim and the examples of content indicated by the R.E. field of enquiry, we have set about showing how the subject can be planned, taught and assessed in both primary and secondary schools. It is hoped that teachers of R.E. will take from this manual all that will be of help when planning their own programme of R.E. in school. To assist them in this we summarise below some of the main points which have been developed in this manual.

It is the task of R.E. to ensure that children have gained some understanding of religion by the time they leave school; that they have explored something of the relationship between religious perspectives and wider human experiences; and that they have reflected for themselves on the relevance of these perspectives and experiences for their own beliefs, attitudes and behaviour.

(Part One)

The field of enquiry sets out the potential range of content which the subject may explore. It comprises three interrelated areas: traditional belief systems, shared human experience and individual patterns of belief. These are not separate static bodies of knowledge, but form a dynamic whole.

(Part Two)

The aim of the subject is achieved through the interaction of children with the teacher and content drawn from the R.E. field of enquiry.

(Part Three)

R.E., like any other subject, depends on an understanding of the fact that teaching must be related to the ability of the children and their appropriate stage of development.

(Part Two)

When the logical structure of the R.E. field of enquiry is linked to insights into the ways in which children learn, a self-evident sequencing pattern emerges. R.E. begins with the observable features of religion and human experience and moves towards those abstract cores of beliefs, spirituality and ultimate questions.

The Systems Approach and Life Themes approach represent different ways of exploring the R.E. field of enquiry. Both approaches remain faithful to the essential nature of the subject, for they enable relevant links to be made between the three areas of the field of enquiry.

(Part Three)

Any topic that is chosen must have potential for exploring an aspect of the R.E. field of enquiry.

(Part Three)

The quality of teaching or the methods of directing pupil learning adopted by teachers are crucial if the subject matter is to come alive and be processed by pupils in a way which genuinely contributes to their learning.

(Part Four)

There is no one set pattern or sequence of activities for all R.E. lessons. Teachers should combine segments which motivate pupils and help them to explore and express faith responses.

(Part Four)

The problem of presumption may be overcome by altering patterns of the statements used by teachers of R.E. It is possible to find ways of speaking which leave them free to state clearly what they believe, what this or that tradition believes and does, without denying to pupils the freedom to respond from their perspective.

(Part Four)

The nature of R.E. is such that it is less concerned with measuring individual gradings than with the way in which children are learning (especially in interaction with each other) and with the benefits they are deriving from it in terms of personal growth and maturity.

(Part Five)

In itself this manual has been concerned as much with how to teach as it has been with what to teach and why it is taught. Supplementry manuals which accompany this general manual explore and explain in detail how and when to teach different aspects of the subject's field of enquiry. They also provide detailed scope and sequence charts related to each religion and to significant Life Themes. In this sense they complement and extend the principles and procedures outlined in this manual.

BIBLIOGRAPHY

Owen Cole, W. (ed.), *World Faiths in Education*, George Allen and Unwin, 1978
Religion in the Multifaith School, Hulton, 1983
Copley, Terence. *R.E. Being Served?*, C.I.O. Publishers, 1985
Copley, Terence and Gill. *First school R.E.*, S.C.M., 1978
Cox, Edwin. *Problems and Possibilities for Religous Education*, Hodder and Stoughton, 1983
Grimmitt, Michael. *What can I do in R.E.?*, 2nd edn, Mayhew-McCrimmon, 1978
Holley, Raymond. *Religious Education and Religious Understanding*, Routledge and Kegan Paul, 1978
Holm, Jean. *Teaching Religion in School*, Oxford University Press, 1975
The Study of Religions, Sheldon Press, 1977
Hull, John. *School Worship – an Obituary*, S.C.M., 1975
New directions in Religious Education, The Falmer Press, 1982
Studies in Religion and Education. The Falmer Press, 1984
Jackson, Robert (ed.), *Approaching World Religions*, John Murray, 1982
O'Leary D.J., and Sallow T., *Love and Meaning in Religious Education*, Oxford University Press, 1982
Rodger, A.R. *Education and Faith in an Open Society*, The Handsel Press, 1982
Schools Council Working Paper 44, *R.E. in the Primary School*, Evans/Methuen Educational 1972
Working Paper 36, *R.E. in the Secondary School*, Evans/Methuen Educational, 1971
Religious Education in Primary Schools: Discovering an Approach, Macmillan Educational, 1977
Sealey, John. *Religous Education: Philosophical Perspectives*, George Allen & Unwin, 1985
Smart, Ninian. *Secular Education and the Logic of Religion*, Faber and Faber, 1968
Smart, Ninian and Horder, Donald. *New Movements in R.E.* Temple Smith, 1975
Sutcliffe, John M. (ed.), *A Dictionary of Religious Education*, S.C.M., 1984
Tilby, Angela. *Teaching God*, Collins Fount Paperback, 1979